Cambridge Elements ☰

Elements in Metaphysics
edited by
Tuomas E. Tahko
University of Bristol

ESSENCE

Martin Glazier
University of Geneva

CAMBRIDGE
UNIVERSITY PRESS

Shaftesbury Road, Cambridge CB2 8EA, United Kingdom

One Liberty Plaza, 20th Floor, New York, NY 10006, USA

477 Williamstown Road, Port Melbourne, VIC 3207, Australia

314–321, 3rd Floor, Plot 3, Splendor Forum, Jasola District Centre, New Delhi – 110025, India

103 Penang Road, #05–06/07, Visioncrest Commercial, Singapore 238467

Cambridge University Press is part of Cambridge University Press & Assessment, a department of the University of Cambridge.

We share the University's mission to contribute to society through the pursuit of education, learning and research at the highest international levels of excellence.

www.cambridge.org
Information on this title: www.cambridge.org/9781108940719
DOI: 10.1017/9781108935494

First published 2022

A catalogue record for this publication is available from the British Library.

ISBN 978-1-108-94071-9 Paperback
ISSN 2633-9862 (online)
ISSN 2633-9854 (print)

Essence

Elements in Metaphysics

DOI: 10.1017/9781108935494
First published online: November 2022

Martin Glazier
University of Geneva

Author for correspondence: Martin Glazier, martin.glazier@unige.ch

Abstract: This Element examines the contemporary literature on essence in connection with the traditional question whether essence lies within or without our world. Section 1 understands this question in terms of a certain distinction, the distinction between active and latent facts. Section 2 steps back to investigate the connections between essence and other philosophical concepts. Section 3 brings the results of this investigation to bear on the traditional question, sketching an argument from the premise that essentialist facts are explained by the origins of things to the conclusion that such facts are active.

Keywords: essence, identity, modality, dependence, explanation

ISBNs: 9781108940719 (PB), 9781108935494 (OC)
ISSNs: 2633-9862 (online), 2633-9854 (print)

Contents

1 Status

1.1 Introducing Essence

Casey Martin is a professional golfer and a coach at the University of Oregon. He suffers from a circulatory condition that prevents him from walking a golf course without severe pain and risk of injury.

In the late 1990s, Martin asked the PGA Tour, a major organizer of golf tournaments in the United States, to allow him to use a golf cart in its qualifying tournament. At the time, the organization prohibited carts and required all golfers to walk the course. Martin's request was denied. He sued, arguing that the organization was legally required to accommodate his disability.

The issue was ultimately adjudicated by the US Supreme Court, which ruled that Martin indeed had to be allowed a cart (*PGA Tour, Inc. v. Martin*, 2001). The court's opinion, authored by John Paul Stevens, justified this ruling in part on the grounds that relaxing the walking requirement would not alter "an essential aspect of the game of golf" (20). Stevens argued that

> from early on, the essence of the game has been shot-making – using clubs to cause a ball to progress from the teeing ground to a hole some distance away with as few strokes as possible. (21)

The use of carts, Stevens concluded, was consistent with that essence.

In his dissent, Antonin Scalia objected that there is no such thing. He wrote:

> To say that something is "essential" is ordinarily to say that it is necessary to the achievement of a certain object. But since it is the very nature of a game to have no object except amusement (that is what distinguishes games from productive activity), it is quite impossible to say that any of a game's arbitrary rules is "essential." Eighteen-hole golf courses, 10-foot-high basketball hoops, 90-foot baselines, 100-yard football fields – all are arbitrary and none is essential. (11)

Scalia's objection faces a number of difficulties. First, games can have objects other than amusement, such as winning prizes or building skills. Second, one may engage in productive activity, such as gardening, for the sole object of amusement. Third, even setting aside objects other than amusement, some rules of some games are necessary for the game to provide amusement. A 1,000-foot-high basketball hoop would not make for a very fun game.

Perhaps most importantly, Scalia seems to misconstrue the notion of essence Stevens has in mind. Scalia is correct that in one ordinary sense, something is essential if one needs it for some purpose. This is the sense in which a passport is essential for international travel. But in speaking of "the essence of the game," Stevens plausibly had in mind a different sense of essence – one which Scalia himself invokes, apparently without noticing. For what Scalia means by saying that "it is the very nature of a game to have no object except amusement" could equally well have been expressed by saying that it lies in the *essence* of games that they have no object except amusement. It is more plausible to interpret Stevens as being concerned with essence in this sense.

Scalia, as we have seen, makes use of this very sense of essence in stating his objection to Stevens. It is therefore especially curious that elsewhere in his dissent it is subjected to mockery. He writes:

> [W]e Justices must confront what is indeed an awesome responsibility. It has been rendered the solemn duty of the Supreme Court of the United States, laid upon it by Congress in pursuance of the Federal Government's power "[t]o regulate Commerce with foreign Nations, and among the several States," U.S. Const., Art. I, §8, cl. 3, to decide What Is Golf. I am sure that the Framers of the Constitution, aware of the 1457 edict of King James II of Scotland prohibiting golf because it interfered with the practice of archery, fully expected that sooner or later the paths of golf and government, the law and the links, would once again cross, and that the judges of this august Court would some day have to wrestle with that age-old jurisprudential question, for which their years of study in the law have so well prepared them: Is someone riding around a golf course from shot to shot *really* a golfer? (10–11)

For Scalia, the question "what is golf?" is "incredibly silly" (11). But evidently he takes a different view of the question "what is a game?" For he purports to answer it: a game is, at least in part, an activity with no object except amusement. In his attempt to dismiss one question of essence, Scalia finds himself offering an answer, however implausible, to another. Essence is not so easily brushed aside.

Essence in this sense (though not, I am afraid, the essence of golf in particular) is the topic of this Element. The concept has a long history in philosophy, going back perhaps even to Socrates' quest for "that form [*eidos*] itself that makes all pious actions pious" (Plato 1997; *Euthyphro* 6e) and running until the burgeoning literature of the present day.[1]

Almost as long is the history of a certain debate about essence. For Plato, "equal things and the Equal itself are … not the same" (*Phaedo* 74c). Since "we … possess knowledge of the Equal before that time when we first saw the equal objects" (75a), the Equal and other forms must apparently reside outside the sensible world altogether. Yet Aristotle objected that "Forms cannot be essences if they are separated, because essences must be intrinsic features of

---

[1] According to Politis (2021), *Euthyphro* 6d–e appears to contain "the earliest occurrence of the term *eidos* when used for the essence of a thing" (50).

things" (Shields 2019: 648, glossing *Metaphysics* 991b1), suggesting a picture on which essences inhabit the same world we do.[2]

The question whether essence lies within or without our world will form our overarching theme. But although the question has deep historical roots, I must leave a comprehensive examination of its history to others. My own strategy will be to draw on the rich *contemporary* literature on essence to gain a clearer understanding of what the question amounts to and how it might be resolved. Along the way, I will chart essence's connections with other philosophical concepts, including identity, definition, modality, explanation, dependence, knowledge, and methodological neutrality.

But before we get there, let me say more by way of introducing the notion of essence. Here are some examples, or potential examples, of essence.

- It is essential to golf to be played with clubs.
- Socrates is by his very nature human.
- What water is is a certain chemical compound, namely H_2O.
- An essential property of gold is *having atomic number 79*.
- George W. Bush is essentially the child of George H. W. Bush.
- What it is to chortle is to laugh in a certain way.
- It is in the nature of God to exist.
- It is true in virtue of the identity of the number 2 that it is the successor to the number 1.

Every example on this list could be challenged. Still, the list demonstrates the potential scope of the notion of essence. There are examples involving the essences of individuals, like Socrates, and examples involving the essences of kinds, like water. There are abstract cases, like the number 2, and concrete cases, like George W. Bush. There are natural cases, like gold, and social cases, like golf.

The list also exhibits a number of different locutions for talking about essence. In addition to "essence," we have "nature," "identity," and "what X is." Although philosophers sometimes seem to assume that these locutions all pick out the same concept, this assumption might be questioned. There might be subtle differences between essence and nature,[3] for instance, or between a thing's identity and what the thing is. Still, it is reasonable to adopt the working hypothesis that these concepts are, if not identical, at least closely related. Most of the time, I will not be too careful to distinguish them.

---

[2] Similar historical points are made by Raven (2021, 2022).

[3] Almog (2010) and Cowling (2013) develop two quite different views on which essence and nature are distinct.

However, there is a different distinction which I *will* be careful to maintain. Suppose that Socrates is essentially human. We may then distinguish two facts.[4]

(1) Socrates is human.
(2) Socrates is essentially human.

Roughly speaking, the first fact "says" that Socrates has a certain property, humanity. Since we have supposed that his having this property is essential to him, let us on this basis say with Raven (2022) that the fact that Socrates is human is an *essential* fact.

While the first fact is essential to Socrates, it does not itself say anything about Socrates' essence. But the second fact does. It says that Socrates is essentially human. With Raven, let us say that the fact that Socrates is essentially human is an *essentialist* fact.

I have just been talking about the essential and essentialist *facts* about Socrates. But is there also something else – some entity we might call the essence of Socrates? There is, of course, the set of essential facts about Socrates, the set of essentialist facts about Socrates, the set of essential properties of Socrates, and so on. Those sets are entities in some sense, and contemporary philosophers have sometimes used "essence" to refer to such things (e.g. Fine 1995a: 275). However, they have tended not to recognize essences as full-fledged entities distinct from sets of essential facts or properties or the like.[5] Lowe (2013), for example, stresses that "it is wrong to think of essences as themselves being *entities* of any kind to which the things having them stand in some special kind of relation" (147). I will follow this tradition here – or at least, I will have nothing to say about essences understood as full-fledged entities.

So much for preliminaries. The rest of this section develops a certain distinction, the distinction between active and latent facts, and asks what the status of essentialist facts is with respect to it. This question offers one way of reconstructing the debate between Plato and Aristotle over whether essence lies within or without our world.[6,7] In Section 2, we step back to investigate the connections between essence and other philosophical concepts. The results of

---

[4] Here, and throughout this Element, I talk freely of *facts*. But the appeal to facts is not crucial and everything I say could also be said without reference to such things (though at the cost of some awkwardness in presentation).

[5] Shimony (1948: 40) is an exception.

[6] I say "reconstructing," not "interpreting." These philosophers may not have been thinking in terms of active and latent facts, but I believe that my question lies in the vicinity of what they were debating and that focusing on it may open up new avenues for progress on the surrounding issues.

[7] A different way of reconstructing that debate appeals to Kit Fine's (2005) distinction between "worldly" and "transcendent" facts. This line of inquiry has recently been pursued in a series of very interesting papers by Mike Raven (2020a, 2021, 2022). Although I have taken a different

this investigation are then brought to bear on our question in Section 3, which sketches an argument from the premise that essentialist facts are explained by the origins of things to the conclusion that such facts are active.

This Element represents the beginning rather than the end of an inquiry. I do not reach a definitive conclusion as to whether essentialist facts are active or latent. Nor do I try to settle many of the other questions about essence which arise along the way. My main aims are to introduce the reader to the contemporary debate about essence, to frame an interesting yet underexamined question about the notion, and to lay the foundations for further work.

1.2 Active Facts and Latent Facts

Facts may be classified as *active* or *latent*. The active facts concern how things are; the latent facts concern how things might be, must be, were, will be, and so on.

The best way to get an initial grip on the distinction is through examples. Here are some examples, or potential examples, of active facts:

- The Eiffel Tower is 984 m tall.
- Hamburg is 300 km from Berlin.
- It is sunny.
- It is not rainy.
- There are tables.
- There are no golden mountains.
- All the coins in my pocket are silver.
- I am conscious.
- Van Winkle is asleep.

Here are some examples, or potential examples, of latent facts:

- The virus could have been contained.
- Nothing can travel faster than light.
- Opposite charges must attract each other.
- Nothing can be both red and green.
- There could end up being a sea battle tomorrow.
- If this match were struck it would light.
- Ivan is irascible.
- Aspirin has the power to treat headaches.
- The earth used to be lifeless.

---

tack here, I have benefited greatly from these papers, and there are many connections between Raven's work and the content of this Element.

- The sun will become a red giant.
- There have always been and always will be massive objects.
- There has never been and never will be a golden mountain.

Although some of these examples could be questioned, I hope that by considering them the reader can get a feel for the distinction. Let us now try to refine our understanding.

The distinction was first drawn by Ted Sider. As far as I know he mentions it in only four places and never discusses it at length. Still, it is well worth considering what he has said about it.

Sider does not use our terms "active" and "latent." Instead, he has offered a number of different characterizations of the distinction over the years. In his (2001: 41) he contrasts "categorical" or "occurrent" properties with "hypothetical" ones (see also Sider 2011: 155n). His (2003: 185) retains the "categorical" and "hypothetical" terminology but adds that the categorical notions are "in a sense 'self-contained' and do not 'point beyond themselves' as the hypothetical notions do." And his (2007: 82) further identifies categorical facts as "manifest."

I think that although these characterizations are not wholly wide of the mark, they are not ideal either. What is the connection between categoricity, occurrentness, and manifestness? Why should the same group of facts exhibit all three properties? And why should those three properties all be opposed to hypotheticality? Moreover, some "hypothetical" facts do not seem hypothetical at all, such as the fact that the earth used to be lifeless.

There does seem to be something right about Sider's thought that the categorical facts are "in a sense" self-contained and contrast with the hypothetical facts, which point beyond themselves. But Sider does not spell out the "sense" he has in mind, and some others, I fear, have been misled. Thus Schaffer (2008) writes:

> Sider provides the following characterization: "Categorical [/occurrent] properties involve what objects actually are like, whereas hypothetical [/modal] properties 'point beyond' their instances." The sense in which modal properties "point beyond" their instances is that they concern what else must be, while the sense in which occurrent properties remain self-contained is that they concern just the actual, intrinsic features of the thing itself. (85)

The bracketed text is Schaffer's, not mine.[8] Schaffer is aware that "this characterization could perhaps use further work" (85), but it is worth saying exactly

---

[8] He has (inconsequentially) misquoted Sider, who has "what objects are actually like."

why. In the first place, Schaffer seems to identify hypothetical facts with modal facts – facts about what might be or must be. Some hypothetical facts, however, are not modal, such as the fact that I used to be a child. (Of course, even this fact *entails* certain modal facts, such as the fact that it is necessary that $2 + 2 = 4$. But since this is entailed by every fact whatsoever, this observation does not help to capture our distinction.) And in the second place, Schaffer seems to suggest that the categorical facts concern the intrinsic features of things. But many such facts concern the extrinsic features of things, such as the fact that Penn Station is subterranean.

Let us therefore leave aside Sider's and Schaffer's attempts to characterize the active/latent distinction and instead seek to clarify it in our own way. One way to do that is to show that it is not the same as various other distinctions. Consider, for example, the fact that it is sunny. This fact, we have said, is active. But not only is it active, it also seems somehow "positive": it concerns the way the world affirmatively is, or features the world decisively possesses. The fact that nothing can travel faster than light, by contrast, is latent. But not only is it latent, it also seems somehow "negative": it concerns the way the world is not, or features the world lacks. Is the distinction between active and latent facts the same as the distinction between positive and negative facts?

No. Although the distinction between positive and negative facts is not perfectly clear, it is clear enough to see that it is not the same as the distinction between active and latent facts. For although it is an active fact that it is sunny, and this fact also seems to be positive, it is also an active fact that it is not rainy, and this would seem to be as clear a case of a negative fact as one could hope for. Or again, although it is a latent fact that nothing can travel faster than light, and this fact also seems to be negative, other latent facts seem more positive, such as the fact that Ivan is irascible, or the fact that aspirin has the power to treat headaches.

We should also resist assimilating the active/latent distinction to the temporary/permanent distinction. It is true that many active facts obtain only temporarily, such as the fact that it is sunny. And it is true that many latent facts obtain permanently, such as the fact that nothing can travel faster than light. But some active facts also obtain permanently, such as the fact that there are no golden mountains. And some latent facts obtain only temporarily, such as the fact that if this match were struck it would light. Once I douse the match in water, this latent fact will no longer obtain.

Some of the examples I gave at the start of this subsection are controversial. The most important controversy for our purposes concerns facts about the past and future. Whether one takes these to be latent will depend on one's metaphysics of time; in particular, it will depend on whether one is an "A theorist" or a "B theorist."

The A theorist thinks there is an objective distinction between the past, the present and the future. The fact that the earth used to be lifeless and the fact that fax machines used to be common, for instance, are objectively alike in that both are facts about the past. And both are objectively different from the fact that the earth is not lifeless and the fact that fax machines are not common. The present moment, for the A theorist, is metaphysically distinguished from all other moments; and correspondingly facts about the present are metaphysically distinguished from all other facts.

The A theorist will take facts about the present, such as the fact that the earth is not lifeless, to be active. They concern how things are.[9] She will take facts about the past and future, by contrast, to be latent. They do not concern how things are but rather only how things were or will be.

For the B theorist, by contrast, the distinction between past, present, and future does not mark out an objective division in reality. The difference between facts about the present and facts about the past and the future, for her, is simply a difference in their relationship to us. Roughly speaking, facts about the present are facts about what is contemporaneous with us; facts about the past and the future are facts about what is earlier or later than us.

The B theorist regards the distinction between the present on the one hand and the past and future on the other in the way most philosophers regard the distinction between *here* and *elsewhere*. On the standard view there is no objective distinction between the objects which are here and those which are elsewhere. The distinction between here and elsewhere is taken to reflect only our perspective on reality and not reality itself. In a similar way, the B theorist takes the distinction between past, present, and future to reflect only our perspective on various objects, events, and facts and not those objects, events, and facts themselves.

When I first introduced the distinction between active and latent facts at the very beginning of this subsection, I contrasted facts about how things are with, among other things, facts about how things were or will be. But we can now see that this contrast is only proper from the standpoint of the A theorist. For only the A theorist recognizes an objective distinction between past, present, and future. From the standpoint of the B theorist, there is no such objective distinction. The difference between facts about how things are and facts about how things were or will be has entirely to do with our perspective on the world

---

[9] Certain facts about the present, such as modal or dispositional facts, may be latent for reasons having nothing to do with their being about the present. I set these aside. Similar remarks apply below.

and not with the world itself. For the B theorist, facts about the past and future are just as active as facts about the present. They are not latent.

Our topic in this Element is essence, not the philosophy of time. Because it will be helpful, for expository purposes, to have a broad set of latent facts to contrast with the active facts, I will sometimes suppose the A theorist's view. But this is only a convenience and could always be dispensed with.[10]

At the beginning of this subsection I glossed the active facts as the facts concerning how things are. But there is a trivial sense in which any fact whatsoever is a fact concerning how things are. The latent fact that the virus could have been contained, for instance, is in this trivial sense a fact that concerns how things are: they are such that the virus could have been contained. So if this gloss is to be of any use at all, we have to understand "a fact concerning how things are" in some other way. But how?

There may be more than one way to answer this question. But a simple answer, and one which is adequate for our purposes, is to adopt a contrastive understanding. A fact concerning how things are is a fact that does *not* concern how things might be, must be, were, will be, and so on. This is not intended as a definition of "active fact." It is only a gloss that, together with the examples and clarifications given earlier, can help us to grasp the active/latent distinction.

Still, the gloss can be clarified further. For there are two ways of understanding it. One is that the active facts are those that do not wholly concern how things might be, must be, were, will be, and so on. The other is that the active facts are those that do not even partly concern how things might be, must be, were, will be, and so on. To illustrate the difference, consider the conjunctive fact that it is sunny and the virus could have been contained. This fact will count as active under the first understanding but not under the second, since although it does not wholly concern how things might be, it does partly concern how things might be.[11] We will understand active facts in the second way. Active facts are wholly active; any fact with even a toehold in the latent is itself latent.

---

[10] Surprisingly, the classification of modal facts as latent is also controversial. For a modal realist like Lewis (1986), what happens in the actual world is ontologically on a par with what happens in any other possible world. The only difference between the actual world and the other possible worlds is that the actual world is the one containing *us*. For the modal realist, the facts about other possible worlds, and hence the modal facts, are just as active as are facts about the actual world. They are not latent. However, modal realism has few adherents. Indeed, the ontological equivalence it draws between the actual and the possible is arguably the central objection to the view. This Element will assume the falsity of modal realism.

[11] The notion of what a statement concerns or is about has recently been theorized in terms of so-called truthmaker semantics (Yablo 2014; Fine 2017b). I shall not pursue in this Element the interesting project of attempting to understand the active/latent distinction in terms of this semantic framework.

A central question of this Element is whether essentialist facts are active or latent. But why ask this question – about any facts, whether or not they are essentialist? Why care?

One reason is reductionist. Some philosophers have thought that the latent facts must reduce to the active facts. Sider (2003) puts the idea this way:

> It is easy to get into a frame of mind according to which modal notions should not be taken as "rock bottom," ontologically speaking. The frame of mind is not unlike Hume's when he confronted causation. One can see the prior event, and also the later one, but where is the causation? Likewise: I can see that this colored thing is extended, and indeed that all colored things I have examined are extended, but where is the necessity, that colored things *must* be extended? Part of the puzzlement here is of course epistemic ... But there is a particularly metaphysical puzzlement here as well. In metaphysics one seeks an account of the world in intelligible terms, and there is something elusive about modal notions. Whether something *is* a certain way seems unproblematic, but that things might be otherwise, or must be as they are, seems to call out for explanation.
>
> Accepting necessity or possibility as a primitive feature of reality would be like accepting tensed facts as primitive, or accepting dispositions as primitive, or accepting counterfactuals as primitive. While some are willing to make these posits, others seek to reduce [latent] notions to [active] notions ...[12] (184–185)

Sider here articulates a view on which the latent facts are taken to be both epistemically and metaphysically problematic. They are epistemically problematic in that it is hard to see how we could know them. And they are metaphysically problematic in that they are not properly taken to constitute primitive or basic or fundamental elements of reality. On both grounds, the problematic latent facts are taken to stand in need of reduction to the unproblematic active facts. So if the reductionist wishes to know precisely which facts must be reduced to which, she needs to know which facts are active and which latent.

But what if one does not embrace this sort of reductionism? Is there any other reason to care about the active/latent distinction? I think there is. For I think that, once we grasp the distinction, we can see that there is a sense in which reality is constituted solely by the active facts.

To see this, imagine that God appears and tells you all the facts about what could and could not have been the case. Thus God tells you that there could have been talking donkeys, and that Biden could not have been a fried egg, and that all those who are actually rich could have been poor, and so on. You

---

[12] I have replaced Sider's "hypothetical" with "latent" and his "categorical" with "active."

would be within your rights to complain: "Well, that's all very interesting. But you still haven't told me anything about reality! Tell me something about how things are, not just about how they could have been." It seems clear that there is a sense of "reality" in which your complaint is justified (if a bit rude).

Of course, God might respond that you are now in a position to deduce some of the facts about reality in this sense. For if you know all the facts about how things could have been (the facts of the form "possibly p" and "not possibly p") then you can deduce all the facts about how things must be (the facts of the form "necessarily p" and "not necessarily p"). After all, it is necessary that p just in case it is not possible that $\neg p$. And once you know it is necessary that p, you can apply the principle that whatever is necessary is true (the modal axiom T) to conclude that p. So, for example, from God's revelation that Biden could not have been a fried egg, you can deduce that it is necessary that Biden is not a fried egg and so that it is true that Biden is not a fried egg. In this way, this and many other facts about reality can be deduced from what God told you. Still, they were not part of what he told you. The facts about how things might be (or indeed about how things must be) are not themselves facts about reality, even though they entail certain facts about reality. Strictly speaking, God told you nothing about reality.

The point stands even if we imagine that God also tells you all the facts about how things were and how they will be (assuming the A theorist's view). Thus God tells you that Caesar crossed the Rubicon and that sea levels will rise and so on. There is a clear sense in which he still would not have told you anything about reality. Of course, in light of this further revelation you will be in a position to deduce many more facts about reality, perhaps even all of them. For example, if God tells you that yesterday it was the case that one day later it would be sunny, you can deduce that it is sunny. That, to be sure, is a fact about reality – but it was not strictly part of what God revealed.

What these considerations bring out is that there is a clear sense in which reality is constituted solely by the active facts. The latent facts, by contrast, lie somehow at a remove from reality. To know which facts are active and which latent, then, is to know which facts constitute reality in this sense.

This is not to deny that there are also senses of "reality" in which reality is partly constituted by latent facts. ("Real" is among the most polysemous terms in philosophy.) For example, we may say that a reality of the philosophy job market is that it is not practically possible for every good philosopher to obtain a permanent position, yet facts about what is practically possible are latent. But that is perfectly consistent with there also being a sense of "reality" in which reality is constituted solely by the active facts.

1.3 Essence: Active or Latent?

What is the status of essentialist facts with respect to the distinction just developed? Are they active or latent? There seem to be considerations which pull in both directions. This subsection discusses some of them. My aim here is not to settle the question but merely to show that it is difficult and worth our attention.

On the side of latency, the essentialist facts can seem to be left unsettled by the facts about how things are. Consider, for instance, the speed of light in a vacuum. It is roughly 3×10^8 m/s, or c. But is this a matter of light's *essence*? Is it essential to light that its speed in a vacuum is c? Does it follow from what light is, its very nature, that it must travel at c? It is hard to say. And so it can seem that, even once we have said everything there is to say about how light *is*, including that its speed is c, we have left open how light *essentially* is. Channeling Sider's Hume, we might say: I can see that light in fact travels at c, but where is the essence?

We must be careful here to disentangle metaphysical and epistemic considerations. One question is whether, if one comes to know all the facts about how light is, one is thereby in a position to know that light essentially travels at c. (See Section 2.5 for further discussion of how we can gain knowledge of essence.) But our concern at the moment is different, and more metaphysical. The thought this example is apt to elicit is that the active facts about light – the facts about how light is – do not include the facts about how light essentially is. Just as some philosophers (again going back to Hume) have seen a metaphysical gulf separating *is* from *ought*, so one might now see a metaphysical gulf separating *is* from *essentially is*. If that thought is correct, then essentialist facts are latent.

Some philosophers might be drawn to say that essentialist facts are latent for a different reason. For these philosophers, essentialist facts are simply modal facts "in disguise." On one traditional modal account of essence, for example, the fact that Socrates is essentially human is just the fact that Socrates is necessarily human if he exists. (See Section 2.2 for further discussion of essence's relation to modality.) If essentialist facts are modal facts in disguise, then since modal facts are latent, so are essentialist facts.

This consideration in favor of latency depends on adopting what we might call a narrowly modal account of essence, an account of essence in terms of the notion of necessity. But even if one rejects a narrowly modal account, one might still regard essence as a broadly modal matter, in the sense that whether a property is essential to some object is a matter of the way or mode in which the object instantiates the property. By analogy, an A theorist might regard pastness as broadly modal in this sense: my formerly being a child involves my instantiating the property of childhood in a certain erstwhile way.[13] In a similar way, one might think that being essentially human involves instantiating the property of humanity in a certain essential way.

One might now suggest that the latency of facts about necessity and possibility is merely a special case of a wider phenomenon. *All* broadly modal facts, on this view, are latent. Thus if the A theorist regards past facts as broadly modal, that will be reason for her to take them to be latent as well. And if essentialist facts are broadly modal, then they too will be latent.

Whatever the ultimate force of these considerations in favor of latency, there are also considerations that pull in the other direction, toward classifying essentialist facts as active. Perhaps the strongest of these, though it is admittedly somewhat elusive, draws on the link between a thing's essence and what the thing is. (See Section 2.1 for further discussion of this link.)

Take water as an example. A glass of water is sitting here in front of me right now. That is an active fact if anything is; to state this fact is to state, in part, how things are. But what is the nature of the water in my glass – what *is* this stuff? The answer is that it is a certain compound H_2O of hydrogen and oxygen. In answering this question I do not seem to have left the domain of how things are and entered the domain of how they might be, must be, were, will be, and so on. I am simply elaborating on my earlier description of the stuff in front of me by stating what that stuff is. Yet what I state is an essentialist fact.

A second consideration on the side of counting essentialist facts as active derives from the connection between essence and sortals (Brody 1980; Wiggins 2001). Consider facts that state which sortal a given thing falls under, such as the fact that Fido is a dog, the fact that Denali is a mountain, or the fact that Orion is a constellation. These facts seem to be active rather than latent; they seem entirely mundane examples of facts about how things are. Yet they might also be taken to be essentialist facts.

It might be objected that an *essential* fact has been mistaken for an *essentialist* one. That Fido is a dog is an essential fact; it has the status of being essential to Fido. But that fact should be distinguished from the essentialist fact that Fido is essentially a dog, which reports that the fact that Fido is a dog has the status of being essential to Fido. The objector might now concede that the essential fact, the fact that Fido is a dog, is active. But she might point out that this does not show that the essentialist fact, the fact that Fido is essentially a dog, is active. And it is the essentialist fact whose activity is in question.

---

[13] Such an A theorist might follow Johnston (1987): "Temporal qualification has to do with the ways individuals have properties. Unproblematically Sam may have the property of being fat in the *t∗* way and have the property of being thin the *t* way. Temporal qualifiers are often adverbs. Sam is presently fat. But he is *t*ly thin" (128).

This objection has some force. Is there any possible response to it? Perhaps. One might grant that there is a sense of "Fido is a dog" in which it states a fact that is essential *to* Fido rather than an essentialist fact *about* Fido. But one might still insist that there is also a sense of "Fido is a dog" in which it states an essentialist fact. Imagine that just beside Fido sits a fantastical shape-shifting creature, Proteus, who can assume the forms of various animals. And imagine that Proteus has just changed from the form of a goat into the form of a dog. Now there is a clear sense in which both Proteus and Fido are dogs. Being a dog in this sense is essential to Fido but "accidental" to Proteus. Yet it seems to me there is also a sense in which only Fido is a dog. For it is only Fido who falls under the sortal *dog*. The fact that Fido is a dog in this sense, it might be suggested, is an essentialist fact. And yet it may still seem to be an active fact. But it has to be said that it is not clear that this response to the objection is successful.

So are essentialist facts active or latent? The answer is far from obvious. And yet the question is of great interest for a number of reasons. Some of these reasons, already mentioned in Section 1.2, are just the general reasons to care about which facts are active and which are latent. But there are also reasons to be interested in whether essentialist facts in particular are active or latent.

One reason concerns the reduction of modality. There has long been a desire on the part of some philosophers to reduce modal facts to nonmodal facts. At the most basic level of reality, these philosophers have thought, necessity and possibility must disappear: fundamental reality is not "full of threats and promises," in Goodman's (1954: 40) phrase. But to which nonmodal facts could the modal facts reduce?

In the mid-twentieth century, some philosophers took the sought-after non-modal facts to be facts about language. It was in this vein that Quine (1943: 121) suggested that a distinctive form of necessity attached to analytic statements – statements like "bachelors are unmarried" whose very meaning ensures their truth. In later decades, however, many philosophers came to doubt that modal facts could be reduced to facts about language. Take Kripke's (1980) example: it is necessary that water is H_2O. Certainly "water is H_2O" is not analytic – one may fully grasp the meaning of this statement without knowing it is true – and it is not clear what other facts about language could account for this statement's necessity.[14]

Might the reductionist have more luck if she looks beyond language? In an influential paper, Fine (1994) proposed a reduction of necessity to essence. The fact that Socrates is necessarily human, on Fine's view, simply arises from the

---

[14] See Sidelle (1989) for one linguistic proposal.

fact that he is essentially human – and similarly for every other fact of the form "necessarily, p." We will discuss Fine's proposal further in Section 2.2, but for now our question is this. Suppose Fine is right. Is this a reduction of the modal to the nonmodal? Or is it merely a reduction of one class of modal facts to another class of modal facts? Have we done away with the threats and promises, or not?

It depends on whether essentialist facts are modal facts. When we say that Socrates is essentially human, are we saying something modal? Or are we just making a claim which, if Fine is right, holds the metaphysical seeds of modality? It is hard to answer this question directly. But one indirect strategy for answering it would be to argue that essentialist facts are active. For it seems clear that active facts are nonmodal: they are facts concerning how things are, not how they might or must be. If essentialist facts are active, then Fine's reduction is a reduction of the modal to the nonmodal.

Another reason to care about whether essentialist facts are active or latent concerns the nature of explanation. (We will discuss the connection between essence and explanation further in Section 2.3.) Some philosophers (such as Kment [2014] and Glazier [2017]) have defended views on which certain active facts are explainable in terms of certain essentialist facts. Perhaps, for example, the fact that water contains hydrogen can be explained in terms of the fact that water is by its nature H_2O. If essentialist facts are latent, then this is a view on which some active facts are explainable in terms of latent facts.

Yet such a view is arguably in tension with the popular "explanatory realist" view according to which all explanation is "backed" by a kind of real or worldly determination.[15] Something in the world makes something else exist or happen and this determination or making underwrites an explanation of whatever it is that is determined or made. For example, if the shattering of this window admits of causal explanation in terms of Suzy's throwing a rock at it, a realist will take this explanation to be backed by some form of causal determination, perhaps the fact that Suzy's throw *made* the window shatter.

Paradigm cases of determination involve one active fact determining another. The fact that Suzy throws a rock is an active fact, and that forces a second active fact to obtain, the fact that the window shatters. This kind of determination is familiar enough.

But if essentialist facts are latent, and if essentialist facts can explain active facts, then the realist view of explanation requires a latent fact to determine an

---

[15] See Kim, (1988, 1994), Ruben (1990: ch. 7) and Taylor (2017) for discussion of explanatory realism. Classic anti-realist views of explanation include the unificationist view of Kitcher (1981) and the "pragmatic" views of van Fraassen (1980) and Achinstein (1984).

active fact. Yet it is not clear that this is possible. How can a fact about how things could have been, or even about how things must be, reach out and force into being some fact about how things *are*?

This subsection has argued that the question whether essentialist facts are active or latent is difficult and important but is also entangled with a number of other issues. We cannot hope to make progress on the question until we have a better understanding of essence's theoretical role and the connections it bears to other notions. It is to this task that we now turn.

2 Connections
2.1 Identity and Definition

One of the most influential discussions of essence in the modern period occurs in Locke's *Essay*. He there glosses essence as "the very being of anything, whereby it is what it is" (III.iii.15), thus forging a connection between the essence of a thing and its identity or what it is. But what exactly is the nature of the connection?

We can start by distinguishing a few different senses of identity. There is in the first place the logical notion of identity: a relation which every object bears to itself and to nothing else. For example, Socrates is identical to Socrates, Plato is identical to Plato, and so on. This does not seem to be the sense of identity most closely connected to essence.[16] For in this sense, while we can speak of the identity relation, or of a thing's identity with itself, it does not make sense to speak of a thing's identity, full stop.

However, there are other senses of identity in which we *can* speak of a thing's identity, full stop. For example, there is one's identity in the sense of who one is or what makes one the person one is (see Olson [2021: §1] for one gloss of this notion). It might be taken to be part of one's identity in this sense to be generous, to be open-minded, to be a philosopher, to be a parent, to be Black, to be a woman, and so on. There is no guarantee that one's identity in this sense will be necessary or even that it will remain the same over time. Consider a fresh philosophy PhD. It may be that, although it is now part of her identity to be a philosopher, this was not the case a decade ago. And, of course, she could have pursued another career altogether, in which case it might well never have been part of her identity to be a philosopher.

---

[16] This is not to say the logical notion of identity is not connected to essence at all nor even that it is not closely connected to essence. Fine (2015) argues that there is "an intimate connection between essence, or the metaphysical notion of identity, and the identity relation, or the logical notion of identity. For to specify the nature of an object *t* is to specify what is essential to an object's being *identical* to *t*" (300).

There is also another sense of identity in which we can speak of a thing's identity, full stop. This is a thing's identity in the sense of what that thing is. Although it is not part of the fresh PhD's identity in this sense to be a philosopher, it *is* plausibly part of her identity to be a human being. Or consider Socrates' singleton set. It is part of the identity of that set to contain Socrates as a member. What this set is, at least in part, is a container of Socrates. A thing's identity in this sense has generally been held to be necessary and to be constant throughout its existence.[17] (The relationship between essence and necessity is further discussed in Section 2.2.)

It is this sense of identity which Locke links to essence. And Locke's thought is still prominent today. Thus Lowe (2013) says that "the essence of something, *X*, is *what X is*, or *what it is to be X*. In another locution, *X*'s essence is the very *identity* of *X*" (145). Lowe also takes up Locke's suggestion that the essence of a thing explains why it is the thing it is:

> Unless Tom has an "identity" ... there is nothing to make Tom the particular thing that he is, as opposed to any other thing. (145)

Fine (1994), in a similar vein, writes:

> [O]ne of the central concerns of metaphysics is with the identity of things, with what they are. ... What is it about a property which makes it bear, in the metaphysically significant sense of the phrase, on what an object is? It is in answer to this question that appeal is naturally made to the concept of essence. For what appears to distinguish the intended properties is that they are essential to their bearers. (1)

Fine here suggests that the fact that a given property bears on the identity of a thing is explained by its being essential to the thing.

An alternative view of the connection between essence and identity is offered by Correia and Skiles (2019). Whereas Fine takes at least some aspects of a thing's identity to be explained by its essence, Correia and Skiles propose that the essence of a thing can be accounted for in terms of its identity. For example (and speaking roughly) they account for the fact that Socrates is essentially human in terms of the fact that being human is part of what it is to be Socrates.[18]

---

[17] The claim that things have their identities necessarily has been questioned by Leech (2018, 2021) and Mackie (2020).

[18] One might think that Correia and Skiles have simply reversed the direction of the explanatory connection recognized by Fine: while Fine explains identity in terms of essence, Correia and Skiles explain essence in terms of identity. But this is not correct. For Correia and Skiles do not purport to *explain* essence in terms of identity but only to give an "account" of essence in terms of identity. Their account takes the form of a certain generalized identity statement (649), and they do not argue that such statements are linked in any straightforward way to explanation.

Closely related to the putative link between essence and identity is a putative link between essence and definition. The latter goes back to Aristotle's remark that "definition is the formula of the essence" (1984; *Metaphysics* 1031a12). But what exactly is the link, and what sense of definition is involved?

We are familiar with the idea that words have definitions: the definition of "vixen," for instance, is "female fox." Let us call this a "nominal" definition. Many philosophers have thought that there is also a sense in which even something nonlinguistic, such as an object or property, can be said to have a definition. These definitions are called "real" definitions. It is natural to state them using locutions like "what it is to be X is to be Y." Thus it might be that what it is to be water is to be the chemical compound H_2O. This is not a nominal definition of the word "water"; after all, people centuries ago knew the meaning of "water" but knew nothing of H_2O. It is rather a real definition of water itself.[19]

There might be cases in which we need to deviate from the form "what it is to be X is to be Y" in order to state a real definition. To see why, consider the following example adapted from Fine (2015: 298) (building on Correia [2006]). Suppose we are doing epistemology and we want to define knowing. One thing we might want to say is that what it is to know a proposition is (at least in part) to believe it on the basis of its truth. But notice that this last claim is not of the form "what it is to be X is to be Y" but rather of the form "what it is to Φ is to Ψ."

One might try to massage the claim into the form "what it is to be X is to be Y," but it is not clear that this will always be possible. And if it is not, then we must recognize at least two categories of real definitions. There are the objectual real definitions, those of the form "what it is to be X is to be Y," which define an object or entity; and there are the predicational real definitions, those of the form "what it is to Φ is to Ψ," which define a predicable.

If there is a link between essence and definition, what exactly is its nature? Some philosophers seem to have regarded the two notions as very closely connected indeed. Lowe (2012a), for instance, holds that "an essence is what is expressed by a real definition" (110) and Hale (2013) that "a thing's nature or essence is what is given by its definition" (151). For these philosophers, it is not just that a thing's definition in some sense provides a formulation of its essence. Essence is itself defined in terms of the notion of real definition.

Other philosophers, even those sympathetic to the notion of real definition, have not wished to go quite this far. Rosen (2015) argues that there may be

---

[19] I do not wish to rule out that linguistic entities might also have real definitions in addition to their more familiar nominal definitions. I will not here consider the interesting question of how the two are related.

things which possess essences, but no definitions. He offers two examples. First, he says it is essential to knowledge that if S knows that p, then p. But he thinks it may well be impossible to define knowledge: just look at the failure of so many philosophers since Gettier (1963) to devise a counterexample-free definition. Second, he says that it is essential to negation that if p then $\sim\sim p$ but that negation is indefinable.

The makings of a response to Rosen's argument are found in Lowe (2012b). Lowe, unlike Rosen, is *inclined* to think that all entities have definitions, but he is "in principle, open to persuasion that some entities are ... 'really indefinable'" (943). His examples, however, suggest a view on which even an "indefinable" entity (if one exists) would have some essential properties and so "admit of *partial* real definition" (943). On this view, Rosen's examples are not examples of things without real definitions of any sort. Rather, they are examples of things which have partial real definitions, but not full real definitions.

If one is further willing to admit the idea that a thing might have a "partial essence" without having a "full essence," then the tight connection drawn by Lowe and Hale can perhaps be maintained. For one can understand Lowe's claim that "an essence is what is expressed by a real definition" as the claim that a partial essence is what is expressed by a partial real definition and a full essence is what is expressed by a full real definition. On this view, knowledge and negation might be regarded as entities with merely partial essences and corresponding merely partial definitions.[20]

In any case, even Rosen is happy to admit *some* kind of link between essence and real definition. But rather than offer an account of essence in terms of defin-ition, he offers an account of definition in terms of essence (200).[21] The account is complex, but the guiding idea is that if what it is to be F is to be Φ, then it will be essential to being F that, whenever something is F, it is F if and only if, and because, it is Φ.

2.2 Modality

Most philosophers have seen a tight relationship between essence and necessity, between a thing's being essentially a certain way and its being necessarily that way. But what is the relationship exactly?

One way into this question is to ask whether there is any entailment from essence to necessity or vice versa. The existentialist Jean-Paul Sartre (2007)

---

[20] Compare Dasgupta (2015: 461–462). I am grateful to referees for suggesting this response to Rosen.

[21] See also Correia (2017b), who offers an account of real definition in terms of generalized identity, a notion Correia and Skiles (2019) argue is closely linked to essence.

is perhaps an example of a philosopher who denied that essence entails necessity.[22] He maintained that "existence precedes essence" in the sense that

> man first exists: he materializes in the world, encounters himself, and only afterward defines himself. If man as existentialists conceive of him cannot be defined, it is because to begin with he is nothing. ... Man is not only that which he conceives himself to be, but that which he wills himself to be, and since he conceives of himself only after he exists, just as he wills himself to be after being thrown into existence, man is nothing other than what he makes of himself. (22)

Although Sartre's meaning in this passage is not perfectly clear, on one interpretation he holds that the essence of a human being is somehow up to that human being, a matter of what she wills or makes of herself. This thought, together with Sartre's famous doctrine that human beings are "condemned to be free" (29), suggests a view on which a given human being was free to will herself to be something other than what she actually willed herself to be, and so on which she could have been other than how she essentially is. On this Sartrean view, essence does not entail necessity: a human being may essentially be a certain way without necessarily being that way.

Most philosophers, however, have not embraced this conclusion. They have instead held that if something is essentially a certain way, then it is necessarily that way (or is so provided it exists).[23] For example, if Socrates is essentially human, then it follows that Socrates is necessarily human (or is so provided he exists). He could not be without being human. Something nonhuman, no matter how closely it resembled Socrates in many respects, would not be Socrates.

What about the entailment in the other direction, from necessity to essence? If something must be a certain way, does it follow that it is essentially that way?

In *Naming and Necessity* (1980), Kripke sometimes writes as if the answer is "yes." He remarks that "some properties of an object may be essential to it, in that it could not have failed to have them" (53). This suggests a certain account of essence in modal terms: what it is for a thing to essentially have some property is just for the thing to necessarily have the property.[24] Clearly, on this account, necessity entails essence: if something must be a certain way, it follows that it is essentially that way.

Elsewhere in the same book, Kripke offers a different account of essence: "when we think of a property as essential to an object we usually mean that

---

[22] Michael Gorman (2014), though he does not deny that essence entails necessity, wishes to leave open the possibility of such a denial. I discuss his view in Section 2.3.

[23] See Leech (2021) for a searching discussion of this principle.

[24] A similar view is suggested by Quine's (1966: 174) characterization of essentialism.

it is true of that object in any case where it would have existed" (48). On this conditional modal account, what it is for a thing to essentially have some property is just for it to be necessary that, if the thing exists, then it has the property. Now if a thing has some property necessarily, then a fortiori it is necessary that, if the thing exists, then it has the property. And so on this account too, necessity entails essence.

This entailment, and the modal accounts that deliver it, were challenged by Kit Fine in his paper "Essence and Modality" (1994). Fine offered a number of arguments, but the most influential of these appeals to an example involving Socrates and his singleton set. (I will present this argument in a slightly different form than Fine does.) It is necessary that if Socrates exists, then he is a member of this set. Thus Socrates necessarily possesses the conditional property of being such that, if he exists, then he is a member of the set. But this property does not seem to be essential to Socrates:

> Strange as the literature on personal identity may be, it has never been suggested that in order to understand the nature of a person one must know to which sets he belongs. There is nothing in the nature of a person, if I may put it this way, which demands that he belongs to this or that set or which demands, given that the person exists, that there even be any sets. (5)

Most philosophers have come to agree with Fine that necessity does not entail essence: an object may have a certain property necessarily without having it essentially. If they are right, then neither of the modal accounts of essence implicit in Kripke (1980) can be correct.

Of course, to show that two modal accounts fail is not to show that all do. Might there be some other modal account, perhaps a more sophisticated one, which succeeds? This is not the place to attempt a comprehensive survey of the modal accounts which have been proposed since the publication of "Essence and Modality." But let us briefly look at a few of them. (My discussion here draws extensively on De [2020].)

Brogaard and Salerno (2013) suggest that "x is essentially F iff (i) necessarily, if x exists then x is F, and (ii) if nothing had been F, x wouldn't have existed" (5). But this account does not accommodate Fine's example of Socrates and his singleton set. For (i) necessarily, if Socrates exists then he has the property of being a member of this set, and (ii) had there been nothing having this property, Socrates would not have existed.

Wildman (2013) suggests that "a property Φ is essential to x iff (i) necessarily, if x exists, then x has Φ; and (ii) Φ is a sparse property" (765), where the sparse properties are "intrinsic, highly specific, carve nature at the joints, and characterise things 'completely and without redundancy'" (763). But this account does not respect the fact that sometimes the essential properties of things are not sparse. The US presidency, for instance, is essentially a public office. Yet given Wildman's characterization of sparseness, the property of being a public office does not seem to be sparse.[25]

Denby (2014) suggests that "x has F essentially iff x has F at every world and F is intrinsic," where "roughly, a property is intrinsic iff its instantiation is insensitive to the state or nature of anything other than its instances" (91). But this account has the disadvantage of being incompatible with origin essentialism, the view that, in at least some cases, the origins of things are essential to them. To take Kripke's (1980) well-known example, the account entails that it cannot be essential to this table here that it originated from a certain block of wood; after all, the property of originating from that block of wood is extrinsic. (Origin essentialism is discussed further in Section 3.)[26]

Given the difficulties faced by these and other modal accounts of essence, it is worth taking seriously the possibility that no such account is correct. That then opens up the potential for a "switcheroo": rather than understanding essence in modal terms, perhaps we should understand modality in essentialist terms. It is just this sort of switcheroo that "Essence and Modality" proposes:

> Indeed, it seems to me that far from viewing essence as a special case of metaphysical necessity, we should view metaphysical necessity as a special case of essence. For each class of objects, be they concepts or individuals or entities of some other kind, will give rise to its own domain of necessary truths, the truths which flow from the nature of the objects in question. The metaphysically necessary truths can then be identified with the propositions which are true in virtue of the nature of all objects whatever. (9)

The basic idea is clear enough. The objects which populate the world have certain essences. For example, it is plausible that Socrates' singleton set essentially contains Socrates and that gold essentially has atomic number 79. Or to put matters in propositional terms, for each object, there are certain propositions which are essential to it. Thus the proposition "singleton Socrates contains Socrates" is essential to singleton Socrates, and the proposition "gold has atomic number 79" is essential to gold. Fine's proposal is that what it is for a

---

[25] A similar objection is raised by Skiles (2015b), who points out that it also causes difficulty for Cowling's (2013) account of the "natures" of things.

[26] A related objection is faced by the account of De (2020), who requires a thing's essential properties to be qualitative – except, perhaps, if those properties concern the thing's constituents in a certain sense. Given origin essentialism, the table has the property of originating from block of wood B. But this property is not qualitative, and nor does it appear to concern the table's constituents in De's sense.

proposition to be metaphysically necessary is just for it to be essential to something.[27]

Clearly, this proposal can be correct only if every necessary proposition has an "essentialist source." Given a necessary proposition, there must be something to which that proposition is essential. But is it clear that this source requirement will always be met?

Some confidence in an affirmative answer comes from considering familiar cases. For example, it is a necessary proposition that water is H_2O. What is this proposition's essentialist source? An answer is ready to hand: water. It is essential to water that water is H_2O. For another example, consider Saul Kripke's claim that it is necessary that he is the child of Myer and Dorothy Kripke. If this claim is correct, a natural essentialist source for this proposition presents itself: the proposition is essential to Saul Kripke.

However, not every necessary proposition can be accommodated quite this easily. What about the proposition that all professors are academics, for instance? It is necessary, but what is its essentialist source? Surely there is no individual professor whose essence requires that all professors are academics. After all, no professor is essentially a professor, and so why would her essence involve professors in any way? Perhaps, then, the source of this necessary proposition is the *property* of being a professor (or an academic).[28] Perhaps it is essential to that property that all professors are academics.

Now this is not an implausible claim. But notice that it does require us to recognize, not simply objects, but properties too, as having essences.

What about logically true propositions, such as the proposition that if it is raining then it is raining ($R \supset R$)? That proposition is necessary; what is its essentialist source? Could it perhaps be *rain*? That seems bizarre. There seems to be nothing about rain in particular that guarantees the truth of this proposition. After all, a perfectly analogous proposition holds for snow, hail, and so on. Rather, the most plausible essentialist source seems to be the conditional connective $\supset$. But notice that this requires us to recognize a logical connective as having an essence.

Indeed, a further expansion of our ordinary conception of essence seems required if the essentialist account is to succeed. Consider the necessary

---

[27] Lowe (2013) defends the closely related claim that "essences are the ground of all metaphysical necessity and possibility" (152). For a quite different account of modality which also appeals to essence, see Kment (2014).

[28] Alternatively, the source might be a certain predicable, being a professor; see Correia (2006). For simplicity's sake, in this Element I will ignore the difference between these alternatives (which is not to say the difference is unimportant). Other potential sources, less plausible in my view, are the concept of being a professor and the word "professor."

proposition that Socrates is distinct from Biden. What might its essentialist source be? Not Socrates, for how could what Socrates is involve Biden in any way? Biden seems wholly irrelevant to what Socrates is. Nor could the essentialist source be Biden, for a parallel reason.

It seems we must say that it is somehow essential to Socrates *and* Biden taken together that the two are distinct. That appears to avoid the problem of irrelevance, since each of Socrates and Biden is presumably relevant to what Socrates and Biden taken together are.

Fine himself does recognize this notion of "collective" essence in addition to the more familiar notion of individual essence. Thus not only is it essential to Socrates – that individual – that he is human, it is also essential to Socrates and Biden – those individuals – that they are distinct.[29]

Once we admit the notion of collective essence, we can better understand Fine's statement of his essentialist account of necessity. He takes a proposition to be metaphysically necessary just in case it is "true in virtue of the nature of all objects whatever." And what that means is that there is some object *or objects* to which the proposition is essential.[30] There must be something in whose individual essence the proposition lies or some things in whose collective essence it lies. (If individual essence is a special case of collective essence, then the first disjunct is redundant.) The notion of collective essence plays a crucial role in Fine's account of necessity.

Hale (2013) has proposed a different sort of essentialist theory of necessity. While Fine endeavored to give a reductive account of metaphysical necessity in terms of essence, Hale's goal is more modest. He defines a special class of metaphysical necessities – that is, a special class of facts of the form "it is necessary that p" – and argues that all other metaphysical necessities can be explained in terms of the members of this special class. What distinguishes this class? It comprises just those necessities which "directly reflect the natures of things" (158). Thus for Hale, although metaphysical necessity cannot be *reduced* to essence, the necessities concerning essence at least constitute a basis in terms of which all other necessities may be explained.

Hale does not view the modesty of his aims as entirely stemming from his own choices. It is, he believes, forced upon him:

> Any true proposition about the nature of a thing – that it is true in virtue of X's nature that $\varphi(X)$, say – is indeed necessary. But its necessity cannot be

---

[29] For further discussion of collective essence and relevance see Zylstra (2019).
[30] Compare Fine's (2000) gloss of his essentialist operator $\Box_F$: "Where A is a sentence and F a predicate, $\Box_F A$ may be read: it is true in virtue of the nature of (some or all) the F's that A" (543).

explained. It cannot be explained by appealing once again to the nature of that very thing, for that would be viciously circular; it cannot be explained by appealing to the natures of any other things, for that would both undermine the claim that $\varphi(X)$ is true in virtue of X's nature, and be viciously regressive; and it cannot be explained in any other way. (158)

Thus any reductive account of metaphysical necessity, according to Hale, must fail for necessary propositions of the form "it is true in virtue of X's nature that $\varphi(X)$." The necessity of these propositions simply cannot be explained.

Hale's argument, however, faces some difficulties. In the first place, it is not clear why explaining the necessity of "it is true in virtue of X's nature that $\varphi(X)$" in terms of the nature of something other than X – of necessity, say, or of essence itself – would undermine anything or be viciously regressive. But to avoid getting bogged down in questions about what undermining is or when exactly a regress is vicious, let me confine myself to addressing Hale's claim that this necessity cannot be explained in terms of the nature of X itself, on pain of vicious circularity.

Consider the proposition that it is necessary that it is true in virtue of X's nature that $\varphi(X)$. Here are two potential explanations of this proposition in terms of the essence of X:

(1) it is true in virtue of X's nature that $\varphi(X)$;
(2) it is true in virtue of X's nature that it is true in virtue of X's nature that $\varphi(X)$.[31]

This is not the place for a detailed assessment of these explanations. The important point for us now is that although Hale thinks that such explanations must involve a vicious circularity, it is not at all clear that he is right. Let p be the proposition that it is true in virtue of X's nature that $\varphi(X)$. Then if we offer the first explanation, we explain the fact that it is necessary that p in terms of the fact that p. There is no evident circularity; these are two distinct facts. And if instead we offer the second explanation, we explain the fact that it is necessary that p in terms of the fact that it is true in virtue of X's nature that p. Again, these are distinct facts and there is no clear circularity. I have not tried to argue that these explanations are free of all difficulty, but there seems at least to be no threat of circularity (vicious or otherwise).

Let me close this subsection by discussing a foundational objection to any essentialist account of modality – or at least, to any reductionist account. The

---

[31] I have elsewhere (Glazier 2017) argued that no "iterated" essentialist claims can be true. But the claims targeted by that argument involved a constitutive notion of essence (see Fine [1995b] for more on constitutive essence). If the explanation in the text is taken to involve a non-constitutive notion of essence, the argument does not straightforwardly apply.

objection, perhaps surprisingly, is due to Fine (2002). Fine (2020b) puts it this way:

> The idea is that a claim of necessity conveys a certain kind of modal import or force and that no account of necessity in terms which lack that import or force can possibly be correct ... (464)

Consider, for instance, the necessary proposition that everything is self-identical. On Fine's way of thinking, part of what is involved in this generalization's being necessary is that there is a sense in which something *forces* reality to conform to it or *prevents* there from being anything which fails to satisfy it.[32] And if essence is not in the same way linked with this "modal force," how could it account for necessity?

We should be clear on exactly what the objection is. The objection is not that we are in possession of some compelling argument that essence does not entail necessity – that, as the Sartrean view sketched above has it, a thing might be essentially some way without being necessarily that way. Nor is the objection that it is unclear what positive argument there is in favor of the claim that essence entails necessity, even if there is also no clear argument against it.[33] The objection as I understand it is rather that (a) a proposition's being necessary is partly constituted by the presence or existence of a modal force, (b) a proposition's being essential is not so constituted, and (c) nothing partly constituted by the existence of a modal force can be explained wholly in terms of something not so constituted.[34] In an admirably forthright recent discussion, Fine (2020b) confesses that "I personally have always been troubled by the issue and am not at all clear what to say in response" (464).

What is it that is so troubling? I cannot be sure exactly what troubles Fine, but here is something that might trouble *someone*. The objection is driven by a worry that essence lacks modal force in the sense of (b) above. But why worry about that? What prevents one from simply embracing the view that essence does have modal force?

Perhaps this. One might take there to be grounds to view essentialist facts as active rather than latent. What grounds? For one thing, one might understand essence as closely connected to identity (Section 2.1): to say that something is

---

[32] Compare Fine (2002: 266) on the force of natural necessity: "in so far as it is a natural necessity that there are no other [natural] kinds [than $K_1, K_2, \ldots$], it is because there is something in the nature of the world that prevents there being other kinds; and the mere fact that there *are* no other kinds can hardly be taken to constitute an adequate account of what this force, or form of necessity, might be."

[33] See Leech (2021) for discussion of this issue.

[34] Mackie (2020) expresses a related worry when she says that one cannot "deliver a modal rabbit out of a non-modal hat" (252).

essentially a certain way is to say in part what that thing is. And facts about what things are can seem to be active (Section 1.3). But if essentialist facts are active, then it may seem that a proposition's being essential cannot possibly be constituted, even in part, by the existence of any "modal force."

These considerations suggest a further reason (in addition to those mentioned in Section 1.3) that the question of whether essentialist facts are active or latent is of interest. If they are active, then the essentialist account of metaphysical modality may have to be rejected – and on the basis of an objection due to its most prominent proponent.

However, our discussion here has been the barest sketch of a certain line of thought. To see whether that line is ultimately compelling will require further work. This work we must leave for another time.

2.3 Explanation

The idea that essence is connected to explanation goes back at least to Aristotle's discussion of demonstration in the *Posterior Analytics* (Charles 2010). A link to explanation recurs in Locke's claim that the essence of a thing is something "whereby it is what it is" (*Essay*, III.iii.15).

In contemporary philosophy, the link between essence and explanation has been developed in a number of ways. One view on which the link is particularly strong is that of Gorman (2005), who defends an account of essence in explanatory terms.[35] Gorman takes the property F to be essential to x "just in case F is (i) a characteristic of x and (ii) not explained by any other characteristic of x" (284). But what does Gorman mean by "characteristic"? He mostly conveys the notion by example. Paleness, for instance, is a characteristic of Socrates. But not every property of Socrates is one of his characteristics. For example, being such that there are infinitely many primes, being a member of singleton Socrates, and being a man-or-mountain are all properties Socrates has, but they are not characteristics of him.

Gorman's account allows essence to be contingent (Gorman 2014: 131). If a thing has some characteristic which is not explained by any of its other characteristics, then that characteristic will be one of its essential properties whether or not the thing has the characteristic necessarily. This openness to contingent essence is uncommon (Section 2.2) and so it is worth noting that it does not seem to be required by the core idea behind the account. As Gorman (2014:

---

[35] A quite different view on which essence is strongly linked with explanation is that of Sullivan (2017), who argues that the essential properties of things are relative to a choice of explanatory framework.

131) notes, the account could be supplemented so as to require that things have their essential properties necessarily.[36]

Disjunctive properties create difficulty for Gorman's account. Can a thing's characteristics be disjunctive? The answer is not clear from Gorman's discussion, but whether it is "yes" or "no," there are problems.

If the answer is "no," then Gorman's account entails that nothing ever has a disjunctive property essentially. But consider the following example from Glazier (2017). Computer programs may contain variables of different types. The types differ over which values their variables can have. A string variable, for instance, can have as its value sequences of characters, while a "boolean" variable can have as its value only 0 or 1. It is not implausible to take the "on-or-off character" of such a variable to be essential to it. Thus a boolean variable foo will essentially have the disjunctive property of having the value 0 or having the value 1. (Of course, foo does not essentially have the value 0, nor does it essentially have the value 1. Indeed, it may have first one value and then the other as the program executes.)

Gorman might try to accommodate this case by saying that characteristics *can* be disjunctive and that foo has the disjunctive characteristic of having the value 0 or 1. But this will not work. For foo's having this characteristic seems to be explained by whichever of those two values it in fact has. If foo has the value 0, that is what explains why it has the value 0 or 1, and likewise if foo has the value 1. Gorman's account will therefore incorrectly entail (by condition (ii)) that having the value 0 or 1 is not essential to foo.

Essence, then, cannot be understood in terms of explanation – at least, not in the way Gorman suggests. Still, the two notions do seem connected. For one thing, many explanations appeal to essences. For example, why is 2 the only even prime number? Well, since a prime number has no divisors other than itself and 1, and since any even number has 2 as a divisor, there can be no even prime other than 2. The facts appealed to in this explanation appear to be essential to being prime and to being even.

In this example, the explanation appeals to essential facts but not essential*ist* facts. Are there explanations that appeal to the latter? Given widely accepted principles of grounding or "in-virtue-of" explanation, there are. This is the form of explanation we give when we explain why Bowser is big-and-bad by saying that he is big and he is bad, or when we explain why the Golden Gate Bridge is red by saying that it is vermilion, or when we explain why this glass is fragile by saying that its molecules are arranged in a certain way.[37]

---

[36] See Correia (Forthcoming) for further discussion of Gorman's view.

[37] Classic works on ground include Rosen (2010) and Fine (2012a). See the articles in Raven (2020b) for an overview of the topic.

It is widely held that a fact f provides a grounding explanation of the disjunctive fact $f \vee g$ (no matter what g is). We have already seen an explanation of this form: the fact that the variable foo has the value 0 provides a grounding explanation of the fact that it has the value 0 or 1. For another example, the fact that snow is white provides a grounding explanation of the fact that snow is white or snow is red.

This principle guarantees the existence of grounding explanations that appeal to essentialist facts: just take the case in which f is an essentialist fact. For example, the fact that singleton Socrates essentially contains Socrates will provide a grounding explanation of the fact that singleton Socrates essentially contains Socrates or grass is orange. But this is a rather uninteresting sort of appeal, since it is merely a special case of a far more general phenomenon: the grounding of disjunctions in their true disjuncts. Are there explanations in which essentialist facts *as such* play an important role?

Kment (2014) develops a theory of grounding explanation in which essentialist facts play a "connector" role in many such explanations (though not all).[38] To get a feel for his theory, consider one of his examples (163). The fact that a certain atom a is a gold atom, Kment says, is explained by the fact that

a is an atom with atomic number 79,

together with the essentialist fact that

it is essential to being a gold atom that all atoms with atomic number 79 are gold atoms.

The role of the essentialist fact is to connect the fact that a is an atom with atomic number 79 to the fact it explains: the fact that a is a gold atom.

Kment also recognizes explanations that appeal solely to essentialist facts (163). For he holds that whenever a thing is essentially a certain way, that explains why it is that way. Or if we countenance "collective" essence (Section 2.2): whenever some things are essentially a certain way, that explains why they are that way.

I too have argued that there are such explanations (Glazier 2017). But while Kment views them as instances of grounding explanation, I maintain that they are instances of a distinctive "essentialist" form of explanation, one not to be understood in terms of ground. I give a few different arguments for this conclusion. The simplest is that it is coherent to take a fact to be essential to

---

[38] Kment uses "metaphysical explanation" rather than "grounding explanation," but I would prefer not to prejudge the question whether there are any metaphysical explanations that are *not* grounding explanations – see below.

something and yet also to be fundamental in the sense of not being grounded in any other fact. A Cartesian dualist, for instance, might hold that a given ego is essentially conscious but that the fact that it is conscious is fundamental. On this view, the ego's consciousness has an essentialist explanation but no grounding explanation. (See Section 2.6 for discussion of the methodology underlying this argument.)

Whatever there might be to say about how essentialist facts explain other facts, they seem resistant to being explained themselves. Consider the fact that it is essential to being even that every even number has 2 as a divisor. Suppose someone asked: why is this? One is tempted to respond by saying something like "that's just what being even *is*." But as Dasgupta (2016: 386) says about a similar example, "in saying this one is most naturally heard not as trying to explain this fact ... in any serious sense but rather as deflecting the demand for explanation."

Whence this resistance to explanation? Dasgupta (2014, 2016) suggests that it may stem from what he calls the "autonomy" of essentialist facts.[39] An essentialist fact, on this view, is in a certain sense inapt for being grounded in any other fact. It is just not the right kind of fact to admit of grounding explanation. And it is because of this inaptness that we find ourselves incapable of answering the question of why it holds.

I myself have offered a different diagnosis (Glazier 2017). I do not think that an essentialist fact, or indeed any fact, is autonomous in the way Dasgupta suggests. What accounts for essentialist facts' resistance to explanation is rather what I call the principle of the inessentiality of essence. This may be roughly stated as the claim that if something is essentially a certain way, then that essentialist fact itself is not essential to anything. For example, although singleton Socrates essentially contains Socrates, there is nothing – not singleton Socrates, not anything else – to which it is essential that singleton Socrates essentially contains Socrates.

This principle entails that there can be no *essentialist* explanation of any essentialist fact. After all, to give an essentialist explanation of an essentialist fact would require finding something to which that fact is essential. And this is just what the principle says is impossible.

Thus while Dasgupta takes essentialist facts to resist grounding explanation, I take them to resist essentialist explanation. If Dasgupta is right, the question of what grounds essentialist facts is closed: they simply do not admit of grounding explanation. But if I am right, the question is wide open. I explore one possible answer to it in Section 3.

---

[39] He does not go so far as to endorse the claim that essentialist facts are autonomous.

Setting aside the question of what essence explains, and of what explains essence, some philosophers have suggested that certain facts about explanation are essential to various things. One version of this idea takes the essences of certain "scientific" properties to include propositions about causal explanation or causation. For example, it might be thought essential to being massive (or to having mass m) that massive bodies play a certain causal role or have certain causal powers: resisting acceleration, attracting other massive bodies, and so on (Shoemaker 1980). Related views take the essences of scientific properties to be given, not by their causal roles, but by their roles in the laws of nature (Sider 2020: ch. 2) or by how objects possessing those properties are disposed to behave (Ellis 2001; Bird 2007).

These "scientific essentialist" views, however, threaten to deliver the uncomfortable consequence that the relevant causal roles, laws of nature, or dispositions are metaphysically necessary. For example, if it is essential to negative charge that negatively charged bodies attract positively charged ones, and if what is essential is also metaphysically necessary (Section 2.2), then it will be metaphysically necessary that negatively charged bodies attract positively charged ones. But most philosophers have thought that the laws governing the interactions of charged bodies are not necessary – not metaphysically necessary, at least – and that negatively charged bodies could have repelled positively charged ones rather than attracting them.

Scientific essentialists have often simply accepted the necessitarian consequence (e.g. Bird 2007: ch. 8) and have attempted to explain away our sense of contingency. However, a more concessive response may be available. On this response, causal roles, laws, and dispositions are taken to flow from the essence, not of the scientific properties, but of the universe itself.[40] It is essential to the universe, the response goes, that it contain certain properties with certain dispositions or causal roles, or that it be governed by certain laws. And this claim does not entail that these dispositions, causal roles, or laws could not have been otherwise. It entails only that they could not have been otherwise in *this* universe. It leaves open the possibility that they could have been otherwise, had there existed a universe distinct from the one we in fact inhabit.

A different version of the idea that facts about explanation are essential involves facts about grounding explanation. The general thought is that when one fact has a grounding explanation in terms of another, there will be some entity or entities involved in those facts to which it will be essential that this grounding explanation obtain. Suppose, for instance, that we explain why a

---

[40] Bigelow and colleagues (1992) develop a related view on which the laws flow from the essence of a certain natural kind, the kind of which our universe is the sole member.

certain ball is colored by saying that it is red. This is a grounding explanation, and one might suggest that it is essential to being red that this explanation obtain. After all, red is essentially a color, and so the essence of being red guarantees that the redness of the ball explains its coloredness.

That is the rough idea; however it cannot be correct as it stands. One reason is that it does not seem right to take the essence of being red to involve this ball in particular. For being red is no more closely connected to this ball than to any other red thing. This suggests that it is not, after all, essential to being red that the redness of this ball explains its coloredness. Rather, what is essential is something more general, something about how redness explains coloredness in general. Rosen (2010) and Fine (2012a) each offer proposals concerning what form this more general claim should take.[41]

2.4 Dependence

Some things appear to depend on others in a certain "constitutive" or "onto-logical" way. A set, for instance, seems to depend on its members, a heap of sand on its grains, a hole on its "host," a shadow on its "caster."

These are putative examples of what one might call individual dependence. A set, for instance, depends on certain particular individuals: its members. We can also recognize a notion of generic dependence. Tahko and Lowe (2020) give the example of electricity. That phenomenon might be thought to ontologically depend on electrons – not on any particular individual electron, but on electrons generally. This subsection will focus on individual dependence.

It was once common to understand ontological dependence in modal terms. For instance, Simons (1987: 295) takes there to be a sense in which one individual ontologically depends on another just in case the existence of the first necessarily entails the existence of the second. Yet he notes two strange aspects of this definition. First, it allows, indeed requires, self-dependence. After all, the existence of any object will always entail the existence of that very object itself. But just as a story of a building can structurally depend on other stories below it but not on itself, we might wish to say that an object can ontologic-ally depend on other objects but not on itself. Second, the definition makes everything dependent on every necessarily existing thing. After all, if a thing

---

[41] Fine would also reject the thought that the more general claim is essential to the property of being red and instead insist that it must be essential to something else. For he holds that the fact that a given grounding explanation obtains (or rather, a generalization of that fact) will always be essential to one or more entities involved in the *explanandum* of the explanation (the fact that gets explained). But in our example, the property of being red appears only in the *explanans* of the explanation (the facts that do the explaining). See Fine (2012a: 76–77) for discussion of this issue.

necessarily exists, then its existence is entailed by the existence of anything else. But it does not seem right to say, for instance, that Socrates ontologically depends on the number 2. For the one object has nothing at all to do with the other. (A related difficulty is that the definition leads to cycles of dependence: for any two necessarily existing things, each will depend on the other.)

In response to these difficulties, Simons defines a second notion of ontological dependence which imposes two additional requirements. First, an individual must be distinct from what it depends on. This prevents anything from depending on itself. Second, when one individual depends on another it must be possible for the second to fail to exist. This prevents Socrates from depending on the number 2 since the latter could not have failed to exist.

But as Fine (1995a) points out, there may well be genuine cases in which something depends on a necessarily existing thing. If sets depend on their members, for instance, then the singleton set of 2 will depend on 2, yet the latter exists necessarily. Our account of ontological dependence should not rule out such cases.

It may be that some more sophisticated modal account of ontological dependence can avoid these difficulties. Nevertheless, philosophers have been moved by them to propose a number of alternative definitions of ontological dependence. This subsection will not survey all of these proposals but will rather focus on accounts that appeal to the notion of essence.[42]

The most straightforward way of modifying Simons's modal account in this direction is simply to replace modality with essence. Rather than take X to depend on Y just in case X's existence necessarily entails Y's existence, we might take X to depend on Y just in case it is essential to X that, if X exists, then Y exists too.[43] Alternatively, we might follow Lowe (2008), who adds to this definition the requirement that it be essential to X that "X stands in some unique relation to Y" (38).

A difficulty for both of these accounts is found in Fine (1995a). Consider Socrates and what is sometimes called his haecceity, the property of being identical to Socrates. (Socrates, of course, is the one and only exemplifier of this property.) One might wish to hold that Socrates' haecceity depends on Socrates. It is standardly held that if a proposition is essential to something, then it is necessarily true (Section 2.2). So if Socrates' haecceity depends on Socrates, the straightforward essentialist accounts entail that it is necessary that,

---

[42] See, for instance, Correia (2005) and Schnieder (2006) for accounts of ontological dependence in terms of the notion of ground. Helpful surveys of ontological dependence include Koslicki (2013) and Tahko and Lowe (2020).

[43] Tahko and Lowe (2020) call this "essential existential dependence."

if Socrates' haecceity exists, then Socrates does too. Yet it is often thought that properties necessarily exist, and so the account entails the seemingly implausible conclusion that Socrates necessarily exists.[44]

Fine himself has proposed a different essentialist account of dependence, one which makes no reference to existence. On this account, one thing ontologically depends on another just in case the second is involved in the essence of the first – or, on Fine's way of regimenting essentialist claims, just in case the second is a constituent of a proposition which is essential to the first. To see the account in action, consider again Socrates and his singleton set. It seems to be essential to the set that it has Socrates as a member. Thus the proposition that singleton Socrates contains Socrates is essential to singleton Socrates, and that proposition has Socrates as a constituent. The account therefore entails that singleton Socrates depends on Socrates.

Does Fine's account avoid the objections faced by modal accounts of dependence like Simons's? That depends in part on how the notion of essence is understood. If essence is itself accounted for in modal terms, then there is at least a possibility that the essentialist account of dependence will turn out to suffer from the same shortcomings that the modal accounts do. But Fine himself has a nonmodal account of essence (Section 2.2). So understood, the essentialist account does avoid many of the objections to the modal accounts. For example, there is no pressure to conclude that everything depends on any necessarily existing thing. On the essentialist account, this conclusion would follow only if the essence of each thing involved every necessarily existing thing, and this does not seem to be the case. The essence of Socrates, for instance, does not involve the number 2.

It might be objected that the essentialist account does not avoid the problem of self-dependence. For it is plausible that a thing's essence will always involve that very thing itself: there will always be some proposition essential to x such that x is itself a constituent of the proposition. The potential examples of essentialist truths given in Section 1.1, for instance, all serve to witness this claim.

But the force of this objection is not so clear. We might perhaps view dependence, like many familiar notions, as coming in "proper" and "improper" varieties. Consider the notion of part, for example. We recognize a "proper" sense of part in which (as a rule) a thing is not part of itself, but we also recognize an "improper" sense in which everything is part of itself. Similarly, we recognize proper and improper notions of subset. We might in just the same

---

[44] Somewhat related considerations are aired by Williamson (2013), who *accepts* that Socrates necessarily exists (or, in his terms, that Socrates is necessarily something).

way recognize notions of proper and improper dependence. We may take x to improperly depend on y if y is involved in the essence of x; we may take x to properly depend on y if x improperly depends on y and x and y are distinct. The essentialist account is an account of improper dependence, but an account of proper dependence easily follows.[45]

Koslicki (2012) argues for a different distinction between two forms of onto-logical dependence. One is "constituent dependence," the sort of dependence an object has on its constituents. (She gives the example of a set and its members: the set in some sense has its members as constituents.) Another is "feature dependence," the sort of dependence an abstraction has on what it is abstracted from. (She gives the example of the particular redness of a given tomato: the particular redness is in some sense an abstraction from the tomato, which is not only red but also round, ripe, and so on.) Both forms of dependence, she argues, may be understood in terms of the notion of real definition. Koslicki herself is concerned to sharply distinguish such definition from essence, but as far as I can tell her accounts of these forms of dependence could also be adopted without too much trouble by someone more open to assimilating definition to essence.

The essentialist account of dependence has been challenged by Wilson (2020). She raises two troublesome cases for the account. Here is a version of one of them. Suppose that one takes quarks to be fundamental constituents of reality. But suppose that one never finds a quark on its own. Rather, one always finds a quark in a pair or in a triple, composing some non-fundamental composite entity, such as a proton. One might propose that it lies in the nature of each of the quarks in such a pair or triple that it, together with the other quarks, composes whatever composite entity they in fact compose. For example, it might lie in the nature of quark q_1 that it, together with quarks q_2 and q_3, composes proton p. Since the essence of q_1 involves p, according to the essen-tialist account, q_1 will depend on p. But on the envisioned view, Wilson says, the situation is exactly the reverse. The non-fundamental proton p depends on its fundamental constituent q_1!

Fine's (2020a) response to Wilson is to distinguish two forms of dependence:

> [T]he intended sense of dependence is one in which the *identity* of one thing, *what* it is, depends upon the identity of another thing. But the sense of dependence to which the above line of argument appeals is one in which the *behavior* of one thing, *how* it is, depends upon the behavior of another thing. (474)

---

[45] A similar defense of Simons's first account could also be given. But such a defense would do nothing to avoid the objection that everything depends on every necessarily existing thing.

Fine argues that it can be true both that q_1 depends on p (in the "identititar-ian" sense) and that p depends on q_1 (in the behavioral sense). Since the two dependence relations are of different kinds, there is no incoherence.

The cogency of this response depends in part on the strength of the case for the distinction between these two forms of dependence. Fine suggests that the behavioral form is to be understood in terms of the notion of ground, but he does not attempt to give a precise account. It would be of significant interest to develop one.

2.5 Knowledge

How do we come by our knowledge of essence? If essentialist facts are modal facts in disguise (Section 2.2), then one way to answer this question would be to "wheel in" an account of the epistemology of modality. Say how we come by our knowledge of necessity and possibility in general, and you thereby say how we come by our knowledge of essence. But the epistemology of modality is a huge topic which lies beyond the scope of this Element.[46] This subsection will focus on proposals for how we gain knowledge of essence that do not go by way of a general epistemology of modality.[47]

So how do we come to know essences? In many cases we apparently do not need to rely on experience. For example, to come to know that velocity is essentially the rate of change of position, we do not need to observe any bodies in motion. Or again, to come to know that the relation of proper parthood is essentially asymmetric, we do not need to assemble or disassemble anything. Of course, experience may be required to acquire some of the concepts involved in these essentialist facts, such as the concepts of position and velocity. But once we have the concepts, we seem to be able to come to know the essentialist facts a priori.

Some remarks of E. J. Lowe might be thought to support the claim that our a priori knowledge of essence is extremely wide ranging.[48] Lowe (2008) writes:

> To know something's essence is ... simply to understand *what exactly that thing is*. This, indeed, is why knowledge of essence is possible, for it is a product simply of *understanding* – not of empirical observation ... And, on pain of incoherence, we cannot deny that we understand what at least some things are, and thereby know their essences. (39)

---

[46] For an overview see Mallozzi and colleagues (2021).

[47] If modality reduces to essence (Section 2.2), then there is at least a possibility that such a proposal can *itself* form the basis for a general epistemology of modality. See Lowe (2012b) for one attempt in this direction.

[48] I am indebted here to Tuomas Tahko (2017, 2018).

Lowe (2012b) expands on the point about incoherence:

> [A]t least in the case of *some* entities, we must be able to know *what they are*, because otherwise it would be hard to see how we could know anything at all about them. How, for example, could I know that a certain ellipse had a certain eccentricity, if I did not know what an ellipse *is*? In order to *think* comprehendingly about something, I surely need to know *what it is* that I am thinking about[49] ... And sometimes, at least, we surely succeed in thinking comprehendingly about something – for if we do not, then we surely never succeed in thinking at all, which is absurd. (944)

For Lowe, the fact that we know anything at all about a given entity entails that we know its essence. But our knowledge of its essence is a product of "understanding," not "empirical observation." This suggests a view on which, for any entity we know anything at all about, we know its essence a priori.[50]

But why should we agree that knowing anything at all about an entity requires knowing its essence? We may grant Lowe that in order to "think comprehendingly" about an entity, one needs to know what it is that one is thinking about. But it is not clear that one needs to know, of the object of one's thought, *what it is* in the sense that philosophers, including Lowe, link with essence (Section 2.1). It may simply be that one needs to have some way of picking out the object, such as by a causal connection or by a definite description or in some other way. And it is not clear why that would require knowledge of essence.

Even if it did, moreover, why should we agree that knowledge of essence is always a product of some non-empirical process of understanding? The thought cannot be that one can come to know something about a given entity only if one *already* has knowledge of its essence, and so that one must already know its essence in advance of acquiring the first bit of a posteriori knowledge about it. For why restrict the conclusion to the a posteriori? By the same token, it would follow that one must already know the entity's essence in advance of acquiring the first bit of *any* knowledge about the entity, including knowledge of its essence. But that is absurd. (Provided, of course, that we *do* acquire knowledge of essence – but in Lowe's view we do, through understanding.)

---

[49] Lowe (2012b) evidently intends a somewhat weak reading of this claim, for he later "concede[s] that a thinker may be able to think of some entity without fully grasping its whole essence" (945).

[50] But Lowe (2014) cautions that "a priori knowledge should not be thought of as knowledge that is entirely independent of experience and as such available, in principle, even to a thinker who has never engaged in empirical inquiry" (257).

Still, we do seem to have some a priori knowledge of essence, even if not for the reasons Lowe gives. When we have such knowledge, how do we come by it? According to Hale (2013), in many cases, our a priori knowledge of essentialist facts can be in a certain way explained by our knowledge of meanings. He gives the following example:

> [A] plane figure is correctly described as "square" iff it is made up of four straight sides of equal length, meeting at right-angles. Precisely because such a definition gives necessary and *sufficient* conditions for the word "square" to apply, there is no mystery how we can know that there is *no more* (and no less) to being square than satisfying those conditions – provided that we are able to recognize the definition of the word as correct, we can tell straight away that being square simply consists in having those properties specified in the definition of the word. (255)

How can knowledge of essence, thus obtained, be a priori? After all, our knowledge of the meanings of words is not a priori. But Hale argues that

> that is no bar to knowledge which draws on our knowledge of word meaning being a priori. For any reasonable account[] of what it is to know a priori that *p* will allow that experience is required to achieve a grasp of the concepts involved in the proposition that *p*, and any plausible account of such concept acquisition will recognize that it is typically mediated by acquiring knowledge of the meanings of some words for the relevant concepts. (255)

For Hale, being square provides an example of the most straightforward kind of case in which a priori knowledge of essentialist facts is explained by knowledge of meanings. In such cases we are in possession of an explicit definition of a word (e.g. "square") whose semantic value is the thing whose essence we wish to know. But he thinks that a somewhat similar account of a priori essentialist facts can be given in other cases.

It was not so long ago that it was possible to believe or suspect that *all* essentialist facts might be knowable a priori (whether in Halean fashion or otherwise). But Kripke (1980) changed all that. For as he pointed out, water is essentially H_2O and yet this fact is knowable only through experience. Or again, gold essentially has atomic number 79, yet this is hardly knowable a priori.

However, it might still be maintained that, in these cases of a posteriori essentialist fact, the "essentialist aspect" of the fact is knowable a priori. Consider, for example, the fact that water is essentially H_2O. It is knowable only a posteriori. Yet it follows from the non-essentialist fact that water is H_2O together with the generalization that any substance with a given composition has that composition essentially (Fine 2012b: 11–13; see also Hale 2013: 259–281).[51] Although the fact that water is H_2O is knowable only a posteriori, it might be suggested that the *generalization* is knowable a priori. And in general, it might be thought that any a posteriori essentialist fact will follow in this way from a non-essentialist a posteriori fact together with an a priori generalization about essence. If this were true, then the "essentialist aspect" of what we know about essence could turn out to have an a priori basis, even if some essentialist facts can be known only on the basis of experience.

But is it really true that *any* a posteriori essentialist fact can be subsumed in this way under an a priori generalization about essence? Consider electrons, for example (Fine 2012b: 12). One might think that an electron is not just negatively charged but essentially negatively charged. This essentialist fact is a posteriori, but under what a priori generalization can it be subsumed? Do not say: anything negatively charged is essentially negatively charged. For far from being a priori, this is not even true! Many things are only contingently negatively charged, such as a balloon rubbed against one's hair.

This example, however, is not completely decisive. As Fine acknowledges, it is at least conceivable that someone might come up with an argument that the following restricted generalization is a priori: any negatively charged *electron* is essentially negatively charged. I might add that it is not altogether clear that electrons *are* essentially negatively charged (though it is certainly not implausible to think so).

The idea that each a posteriori essentialist fact is subsumable under an a priori generalization about essence might be reassuring to someone who was sanguine about the possibility of a priori knowledge of essence. But what about someone who is not so sanguine? She will feel some attraction to epistemological skepticism about essence unless she has a reason to think we can gain evidence for essentialist facts without relying on a priori claims about essence.

Just such a reason is offered by Kment (2021). As we saw in Section 2.3, for Kment (2014) essentialist facts play a distinctive role in grounding or in-virtue-of explanation. For example, the fact that it is essential to being a gold atom that all atoms with atomic number 79 are gold atoms will constitute part of a grounding explanation of why this atom here is a gold atom. Now in general, explanatory claims can gain evidential support from their figuring in a theory

---

[51] The idea that the essentialist aspect of an a posteriori essentialist fact is knowable a priori has a counterpart in the literature on the necessary a posteriori. The thought there is that the a posteriori fact that water is necessarily H_2O follows from the nonmodal fact that water is H_2O together with the generalization that any substance with a given composition has that composition necessarily, or some similar generalization. And so the modal aspect of an a posteriori necessity fact is knowable a priori. See Burgess (2020) for discussion.

that possesses various virtues like simplicity, strength, and so on. A sufficiently comprehensive theory, for Kment, will include claims about grounding explanation and so will thereby include claims about essence. He therefore concludes that claims about essence can be supported abductively, through playing a role in an attractive theory.

2.6 Neutrality

How important is essence to the discipline of metaphysics? Not very, says Ted Sider (2011): "Metaphysics, at bottom, is … [n]ot about what properties are essential" (1). Hugely, says Kit Fine (2017a): "[M]etaphysics in general is concerned with the nature of things" (101). These disagreements over the aims of metaphysics naturally beget disagreement over metaphysical methodology. If essence is central to metaphysical inquiry, then presumably we should do metaphysics always with an eye to essentialist considerations; if not, not.

Vital though they are, these big questions about the aims of metaphysics lie beyond the scope of this Element. In this subsection I wish instead to discuss a smaller question of metaphysical methodology which I believe essence may also be able to illuminate: the question of neutrality.

To discuss this question clearly, we will need to consider examples of how philosophers have relied upon, or dismissed, considerations of neutrality when conducting metaphysical debates. The content of these debates, however, is largely irrelevant. We are interested in them only for what light they can shed on the question of neutrality. In what follows, I will not provide extensive commentary on or explication of the content of the debates I discuss. I will try to say just enough so that our methodological investigation can proceed.

Let us begin with a passage from a recent paper on time and modality by Dorr and Goodman (2020).

> We are not claiming that it is an important desideratum that a view be *neutral* as regards hypotheses like [the two propositions we just stated]; on the contrary, we see settling such difficult questions as an advantage of a theory about time and modality. In metaphysics as in other areas of theory-building, strength is a virtue. (657)

They are not alone in rejecting the methodological importance of neutrality. A decade earlier, in a book on fundamentality, Sider (2011) wrote:

> Neutrality on "first-order" questions like [the one I just raised] is not a reasonable constraint on the metaphysics of fundamentality. A metaphysics of fundamentality is supposed to give the truth about the nature of fundamentality, not provide a dialectically neutral framework in which to conduct first-order debates. (136)

And earlier still, Lewis (1986) declared that "metaphysical neutrality is not among my aims" (105n2).

Others, however, *have* aimed at neutrality. Thus Amijee (2021) writes:

> Second-order claims (i.e. the claims that state constraints on metaphysical explanation) ought to be ecumenical with respect to a sufficiently broad range of first-order claims (i.e. the claims that merely employ the notion of explanation). (1172)

And Wilson (2020), in a discussion of Fine's "Essence and Modality" (1994), approvingly characterizes him as

> concerned not to push any particular line as regards what is essential to what but rather to make room for any "intelligible" conception of these matters. (285)

As these examples make clear, contemporary metaphysicians are divided over the question of the methodological importance of neutrality. What is not so clear, however, is exactly what this question amounts to and what the considerations relevant to settling it might be.

This is not the place to attempt a comprehensive treatment of these issues. But I would like to propose a principle which I believe may lie at the heart of the divide evidenced above. If the principle is true, a certain form of neutrality has obvious methodological importance; if it is false, neutrality may be of little or no importance. I will sketch an argument for the principle that appeals crucially to essentialist considerations. I am not sure the argument succeeds, but I think it is worth taking seriously.

The principle is best developed by returning to the passage in "Essence and Modality" which is Wilson's focus in the above quotation. It appears following the "singleton Socrates" counterexample to the modal account of essence (Section 2.2). Fine (initially) wields the counterexample against the conditional version of the modal account, according to which what it is for a thing to essentially have some property is just for it to be necessary that, if the thing exists, then it has the property. His complaint is that because it is necessary that, if Socrates exists, then he is a member of singleton Socrates, this modal account entails that Socrates is essentially a member of singleton Socrates – and yet intuitively this last claim is false. After presenting a second, related counterexample, Fine writes:

> Nor is it critical to the example that the reader actually endorse the particular modal and essentialist claims to which I have made appeal. All that is necessary is that he should recognize the intelligibility of a position which makes such claims. For any reasonable account of essence should not be biased

towards one metaphysical view rather than the other. It should not settle, as a matter of definition, any issue which we are inclined to regard as a matter of substance. (5)

For Fine, the bare "intelligibility" of a certain position – namely, the position that although Socrates is necessarily a member of singleton Socrates if he exists, he is not essentially a member of singleton Socrates – is enough to establish the falsity of the conditional modal account.

Fine does not in this passage say exactly how he wishes to understand the notion of intelligibility. He does seem to suggest that a position (or a claim which that position makes) will be intelligible just in case the question whether it is true is "a matter of substance," but that is not of much help. We might perhaps fill out the notion slightly by requiring an intelligible claim to at least be coherent and somewhat plausible (cf. Fine 2013: 728). But a fuller characterization of intelligibility must await another time.

Let us suppose – if we can! – that this notion of intelligibility is clear enough to be getting on with. We may then ask: what exactly is Fine's argument in the above passage from "Essence and Modality"? Let p be the conjunctive claim that (a) Socrates is necessarily a member of singleton Socrates if he exists and (b) Socrates is not essentially a member of singleton Socrates. Here is a reconstruction of the argument:

(1) The conditional modal account of essence entails the falsity of p.
(2) It is intelligible that p.
(3) If an account of essence entails the falsity of an intelligible claim, then the account is false.
(4) So the conditional modal account of essence is false.

The first premise is clearly true, and let us grant Fine that, despite the unclarity of the notion of intelligibility, the second premise is true as well. Why should we accept the third premise?

One might try to argue for it on the basis of a very general principle of neutrality, such as the principle that, if some philosophical claim entails the falsity of an intelligible claim, then that philosophical claim is false. But even setting aside the vagueness of "philosophical claim," this principle is far too strong. Let (ethical) vegetarianism be the view that eating meat is wrong. Then it is a philosophical claim that vegetarianism is true. And it is surely an intelligible claim that vegetarianism is false. But although the philosophical claim that vegetarianism is true entails the falsity of the intelligible claim that vegetarianism is false, that is hardly grounds for rejecting vegetarianism!

A second principle of neutrality is inspired by the passage from Amijee quoted above: if some second-order claim about a given notion (a claim which states a constraint on the notion) entails the falsity of an intelligible first-order claim about that notion (an intelligible claim which merely employs the notion), then the second-order claim is false.[52]

One might quibble here with Amijee's distinction between first- and second-order claims. After all, any claim whatsoever about some notion states some sort of constraint on it – the notion is constrained to be such that the claim is true – and so there is pressure to take all claims to be second-order. But set this worry aside. Even if a distinction between first- and second-order claims can be made out, the principle appears subject to counterexample.

Consider the claim that the physical is causally closed: a physical event cannot have a non-physical cause. This claim states a constraint on causation if anything does, and so it will presumably count as a second-order claim about causation. And it is an intelligible first-order claim about causation that a certain change in my immaterial soul just now caused me to dance. The second-order claim entails the falsity of the first-order claim, and yet that entailment does not seem to constitute a reason to reject the causal closure of the physical.

I suggest that we would do better to consider Fine's remark that an account of essence "should not settle, as a matter of *definition*, any issue which we are inclined to regard as a matter of substance." This remark suggests a third principle of neutrality: if some putative (real) definition entails the falsity of an intelligible claim, then that putative definition is false. If we now understand an "account" of something as a putative definition of it, then this third principle entails our third premise: if an account of essence entails the falsity of an intelligible claim, then the account is false. And it does not fall prey to the counterexamples raised above, since neither the claim that vegetarianism is true nor the claim that the physical is causally closed are putative definitions.

Still, why believe the third principle? Here is a suggestion. When a claim is intelligible, we are in a position to know that its truth is consistent with the essences or natures of the items it involves. For example, consider again the claim that a certain change in my immaterial soul caused me to dance. It is intelligible. And the suggestion is that merely by appreciating its intelligibility, we can come to know that its truth is consistent with the natures of the items it involves, such as my soul and dancing and causation. Even if my dancing is not in fact caused by a change in my soul, there is at least no incoherence

---

[52] As it stands the third premise applies to any intelligible claim and is thus too broad to be supported by this principle. But the argument would not suffer if the third premise were modified to apply only to intelligible first-order claims about essence.

in the claim that it is. But if the very nature of dancing (say) entailed that my dancing could not be caused by a change in my soul, then there *would* be such an incoherence. Thus any account of dancing which entails that my dancing is not so caused must be false. (I assume the account will take the form of a real definition. The argument does not straightforwardly apply to accounts of other kinds.)

The third principle, however, is still subject to counterexample. It is a putative account of water – indeed, a true account – that it is H_2O. And it is an intelligible claim – or was, in centuries past – that water is not H_2O but rather has some other chemical composition XYZ. The account of water as H_2O entails the falsity of the claim that water is XYZ. Yet that is no reason to reject the account.

The problem is that our suggestion in support of the third principle was too strong. It is not true that whenever a claim is intelligible, we are in a position to know that its truth is consistent with the natures of the items it involves. Centuries ago, the claim that water is XYZ was intelligible, yet we were not in a position to know that its truth was (in)consistent with the nature of water. Why not? Because the nature of water is not knowable a priori. Its discovery required empirical investigation. But if we restrict our attention to items whose natures *are* knowable a priori, then our suggestion has some plausibility: whenever a claim is intelligible, we are in a position to know that its truth is consistent with the natures of the items it involves, provided those natures are knowable a priori.

This thought supports a fourth (and final) principle of neutrality.

Neutrality.   If a putative definition of something whose essence is knowable a priori entails the falsity of an intelligible claim, then that putative definition is false.

This principle has clear methodological ramifications. In particular, in attempting to give (definitional) accounts of things whose essences are knowable a priori, we should be concerned to make room for any intelligible conception of those things.

As far as I can tell there is no guarantee that the items we wish to give such accounts of in philosophy will always have essences that are knowable a priori. Still, it seems that for a great many philosophical notions, experience is of little help in discovering their essences. And so, if these essences are knowable at all, they are knowable a priori. So if we adopt the working assumption that the essences of these things are knowable (for otherwise it would make little sense to offer accounts of them) then given Neutrality we should also adopt the working assumption that, if an account of one of these things entails the falsity of an intelligible claim, then that account is false. Accounts of such things should make room for any intelligible conception of their targets.

3 Origins

3.1 What Grounds Essences?

In this section we return to the question, first raised in Section 2.3, of what the metaphysical grounds of essentialist facts might be. What do such facts hold in virtue of? Where do they come from, metaphysically speaking? How do they get to obtain? This section develops one possible answer to this question and explores what light it can shed on the issue of whether essentialist facts are active or latent.

For many categories of fact, we can say something interesting and general about what grounds them. Thus (suppressing some details) the conjunctive fact $A \wedge B$ is grounded in its conjunct facts A and B taken together. The disjunctive fact $A \vee B$ is grounded in the fact that A or in the fact that B, whichever one obtains (or in each one separately, if both obtain). The universal fact $\forall x F x$ is grounded in the fact that Fa, the fact that Fb, and so on for all the objects there are (plus, perhaps, the fact that there are no other objects). The existential fact $\exists x F x$ is grounded in the fact that Fa or in the fact that Fb or in the fact that Fc ..., whichever one obtains (or in several of these facts taken separately, if several of them obtain). Determinable facts like "a is red" are grounded in determinate facts like "a is crimson." And on and on.[53]

What about essentialist facts? What grounds *them*?

In attempting to answer this question we immediately confront a certain choice point. We have seen that some philosophers have defended accounts of essence in modal terms (Section 2.2). On these accounts, the question of what grounds essentialist facts will be answered in large part by answering the question of what grounds modal facts.

But this strategy for grounding essentialist facts faces two difficulties, one principled and one practical. The practical difficulty is that it is not at all clear what grounds modal facts (Cameron 2010). Thus it is not as if there are grounds for essentialist facts ready to hand if only we would adopt a modal account of them. And the principled difficulty is that there are reasons to doubt the modal account (Section 2.2). Although I have not attempted in this Element to argue that these reasons are decisive, I myself believe they are. I will therefore assume in this section that essence is not to be understood in modal terms. Those with

---

[53] For more discussion of these and other cases see Rosen (2010) and Fine (2012a).

more sympathy for the modal account may take this as an invitation to consider what might ground essentialist facts given that account.

But one may now worry that the question of what grounds essentialist facts rests on a false presupposition. For is it even clear that these facts *have* grounds? Perhaps they are simply metaphysically rock bottom or fundamental, in the sense of being ungrounded by any other fact.

Essentialist facts are not fundamental facts in this sense. Or at least, it is plausible that many essentialist facts are not fundamental. For there are presumably many things that form no part of fundamental reality. Consider, for example, the Hamburg Stadtpark, the cloud currently overhead, or the US presidency. Presumably, no description of fundamental reality will make reference to these things. They are, we might say, purely derivative entities. Yet all the same there seem to be essentialist facts about them: the Stadtpark is essentially a park; the cloud overhead essentially contains water; the US presidency is essentially a public office. If these things are not part of fundamental reality, and if there are essentialist facts about them, then these essentialist facts cannot be fundamental facts.[54]

The point does not depend on these particular examples. As long as there are some things that are not part of fundamental reality but that nevertheless have essences, the essentialist facts about those things cannot be fundamental. If one insists on taking all essentialist facts to be fundamental, it will be hard to maintain the distinction between what is and is not part of fundamental reality. We will face an implausible proliferation of what one might call the "ultimate furniture of the universe."

It might be suggested that a thing should count as being part of fundamental reality only if the fact that it *exists* is fundamental. The mere obtaining of fundamental *essentialist* facts about the thing will then do nothing to "bloat" fundamental reality. But the problem with this suggestion is that it is not clear what is so special about existence facts. Let a thing be fundamentally existent or let it be fundamentally F, whatever F is: the thing plays a role in fundamental reality either way.

So, many essentialist facts are not fundamental facts. There must therefore be some facts that ground them. What could these be?

3.2 The Origins Proposal

I will explore a proposal for how essentialist facts might be grounded. I am not convinced that the proposal is correct. But I do think it can overcome

---

[54] This argument is developed in more detail in Glazier (2017); I here ignore certain subtleties for the sake of a streamlined presentation.

some seemingly strong objections and that it merits serious consideration. The proposal is that essentialist facts are grounded in facts about the origins of things.

I am far from the first to suggest that there might be a link between essence and origin. Kripke (1980) gave several well-known examples of what he took to be cases in which a thing's origins are essential to it. Here are two of his best-known cases. First, a certain table T, which on January 29, 1970, furnished a lecture hall at Princeton, essentially originated from a certain block of wood B. Second, Queen Elizabeth II essentially originated from a certain sperm s and egg e.[55]

Kripke also offered an argument for the general principle that "if a material object has its origin from a certain hunk of matter, it could not have had its origin in any other matter" (114n).[56] Of course, this principle concerns modality and not essence (assuming the modal account of essence is false). Still, if anything like this principle is correct, that at least suggests that there might be a general link between essence and origin.

The connection between essence and origin may be even tighter than Kripke thought. Suppose he is right that the Princeton table T essentially originated from the block of wood B; why should this be so? It does not seem obviously wrong to answer: that's how the table was made. Put another way, it is in T's nature to have come from B because T was made from B. And this suggests a view on which the fact that T essentially originated from B is grounded in the fact that T originated from B.

The idea that essences might somehow be explained by origins has been explored in the work of Joseph Almog (1989, 1991, 1996, 1999, 2003, 2010). Almog (2003: 209) characterizes his view this way: "My own theoretical account traces the forging of [something's] essential traits to the generative process by which [it] came into being." For Almog, there is a kind of explanation that may be given of something's essence in terms of its generation or origins.

Let an origin fact about t be any fact of the form "t originated from $s_1, \ldots, s_n$." Although Almog himself does not explicitly cast his view in terms of the notion

---

[55] As Robertson (1998: 732n) points out, Kripke does not put forward exactly these essentialist claims. For example, he asks rhetorically, "Now could *this table* have been made from a completely *different* block of wood" – and the answer is meant to be "no." This leaves it open that the table could have been made from a not-completely-different block of wood, perhaps one differing from B by only a few atoms, and so that it is not the case that T essentially originated from B but only from what one might call a B-variant (Hawthorne and Gendler 2000: 290). For present purposes we can safely ignore the differences between these essentialist claims.

[56] The argument is controversial. For discussion, see Salmon (1979), Rohrbaugh and deRosset (2004), Cameron (2005), Damnjanovic (2010), Ballarin (2013), and Hale (2013: 264–266).

of ground, one might, inspired by his view, propose the following very general "Almogian" grounding thesis: for all t and A, if t is essentially such that A, then the fact that t is essentially such that A is grounded in origin facts about t.[57,58]

Such a sweeping claim carries the interest and excitement characteristic of big, bold metaphysical theses – and also the potential for overreach. Two immediate concerns arise.

First, there is a difficulty involving objects which lack origins. Consider the number 2, for instance; it is essentially prime. If the Almogian thesis is correct, then the fact that 2 is essentially prime must be grounded in origin facts about 2. But we do not standardly think that 2 has origins. Numbers on the standard view are abstract objects and do not come into being in the way that a tree or a car do.

Second, there is a difficulty involving essentialist facts which have nothing to do with origins. Consider the fact that water is essentially H_2O. Given the Almogian thesis, this fact is grounded in facts about water's origins. Now unlike the number 2, water *does* have origins, at least in the sense that there was a moment at which the first quantity of water came into existence. Still, one might think that whether a substance is H_2O has to do only with its current composition and not with its origins. And so one might hold that the origins of water are irrelevant to its being essentially H_2O. Since grounds must be relevant to what they ground, the Almogian thesis is false.

It is not clear to me that these difficulties are insurmountable. To meet the first difficulty, one could try to argue that, despite appearances, all objects with essences do have origins (on a sufficiently broad construal of "origins"). Take the number 2, for example; Raven (2021: 1061) floats a view on which "mathematical objects are produced by processes involving the activities of mathematicians." And to meet the second difficulty, one could try to argue that a thing's origins *are* after all relevant to every essentialist fact about it. Take water, for example; one might try to argue that its being H_2O is a matter not of its current composition but of its being identical to the chemical compound H_2O and that this is indeed connected to its origins.

Whether these or other responses can be made to work is not something I want to try to settle here. Instead I prefer to consider a far narrower grounding proposal that avoids the difficulties faced by the Almogian thesis.

---

[57] Raven (2021) discusses a related Almogian thesis, perhaps one closer to Almog's own view.

[58] If we admit cases of collective essence (Section 2.2), then we should extend this thesis to accommodate them: if $t_1, \ldots, t_n$ are essentially such that A, then the fact that $t_1, \ldots, t_n$ are essentially such that A is grounded in origin facts about $t_1, \ldots, t_n$. However, admitting such cases would make no difference to the arguments of this section and so for simplicity's sake I will ignore them.

Origins proposal.   If t essentially originated from $s_1,\ldots,s_n$, then the fact that t essentially originated from $s_1,\ldots,s_n$ is grounded in the fact that t originated from $s_1,\ldots,s_n$.

There is now no longer any difficulty involving objects without origins since the proposal applies only to essentialist facts about objects *with* origins. And there is no longer any difficulty involving essentialist facts having nothing to do with origins, since the proposal applies only to essentialist facts *about* origins. Additionally, because the proposal is a conditional claim, it does not presuppose that there even *is* anything which has its origins essentially.

Although the origins proposal is narrower than the sweeping Almogian thesis, it remains of significant interest. For one may worry that essentialist facts are in principle incapable of being grounded. We saw in Section 2.3 that Dasgupta (2014, 2016) has raised worries of this kind. If the origins proposal can be sustained, those worries are laid to rest.

3.3 The Circularity Objection

The origins proposal appears to face a serious objection. The objection is that the proposal leads to circular explanation.

To understand the objection, consider again the Princeton table T. According to the origins proposal, the fact that T essentially originated from B is grounded in the fact that T originated from B. There is thus a kind of explanation that can be given of the former in terms of the latter.

Yet there is also a kind of explanation running in the other direction. For in general, if something is a certain way by its very nature, that seems sufficient to explain why it is in fact that way. After all, it has to be that way if it is to be the thing that it is. There is no other way for *it* to be. And so the fact that T essentially originated from B provides a kind of explanation of the fact that T originated from B.

We therefore have an explanatory circle. The fact that T essentially originated from B explains why T originated from B, which in turn explains why T essentially originated from B.

To see how the defender of the origins proposal can respond to this charge of circularity, it will help first to consider a similar circularity objection that has recently received significant attention. This is the circularity objection to the Humean view of laws of nature. It will be instructive to examine how the debate over this objection has played out over the past decade. (I will ignore certain subtleties as only the broad contours of the debate are relevant to our present concerns.)

The Humean holds that laws of nature are nothing other than regularities.[59] Consider, for instance, a putative law of ornithology to the effect that ravens must be black. For the Humean, this law is nothing other than the regularity that, in point of fact, each and every raven is black.

Humeanism faces the following objection. A regularity is explained, at least in part, by its instances. For instance, the regularity that all ravens are black is explained by its instances: this raven's being black, that raven's being black, and so on. Put all those instances together and you have at least a partial explanation for the regularity.[60] Yet the instances may themselves be explained, at least in part, in terms of the ornithological law that ravens must be black. Take any individual raven; it is black, at least in part, because of the law. And if, as the Humean says, the law that ravens must be black is nothing other than the regularity that all ravens are black, then we have an explanatory circle: the law explains or helps explain the instances, which in turn explain or help explain the law.

This objection to Humeanism goes back at least to Armstrong (1983) (see also Maudlin 2007) but in his (2012) Loewer offered an innovative and influential response. Loewer suggested that the explanation of the law in terms of its instances is what he called a "metaphysical" explanation, while the explanation of the instances in terms of the law is a "scientific" explanation. Because the two halves of the explanatory circle involve different forms of explanation, the circle is unproblematic.

A reply to Loewer was soon given by Lange (2013). Lange was happy to agree with Loewer that the explanatory circle involves two different forms of explanation, metaphysical and scientific. But he insisted that that point alone was not enough to dissolve the circularity objection. For Lange argued that a metaphysical explanation, when "chained" with a scientific explanation, yields a further *scientific* explanation. Thus if one takes the metaphysical explanation of the law in terms of the instances, and if one chains that with the scientific explanation of the instances in terms of the law, one obtains a scientific explanation of the instances in terms of themselves. This violates the principle that explanations must be irreflexive: nothing explains or helps explain itself. And so Loewer's distinction between two forms of explanation, Lange concluded, does not free the Humean from circularity.

---

[59] For Humeans, all laws of nature are regularities, but not all regularities are laws of nature. What distinguishes those regularities which are laws from those which are not? Lewis (1973) offered an influential answer: the laws are the regularities that form part of the "best system."

[60] To get a full explanation one might need to appeal to the fact that there are no ravens other than the ones involved in these instances.

Lange's proposed chaining principle was soon challenged, and the debate over the circularity objection continued.[61] But we need not follow its twists and turns any further. What matters for us is that the defender of the origins proposal, who also faces a circularity objection, can offer a response to that objection that is analogous to Loewer's.

Recall how the objection goes. The fact that T essentially originated from B explains why T originated from B, which in turn explains why T essentially originated from B. We have seen that, faced with a similar circularity, Loewer argued that the two halves of the circle involved two different forms of explanation: "metaphysical" and "scientific." The defender of the origins proposal may respond in just the same way. She may insist that the first half of her circle involves an *essentialist* explanation, while the second involves a *grounding* explanation. The fact that T essentially originated from B provides an essentialist explanation of why T originated from B, while the fact that T originated from B provides a grounding explanation of why T essentially originated from B. The defender of the origins proposal may now suggest that, because the two halves involve different forms of explanation, the circle is unproblematic.

One possible reply to this response is to challenge the claim that these are two different forms of explanation. In particular, one might insist that both halves of the circle are grounding explanations. According to this reply, the reason one can explain the fact that something is a certain way in terms of the fact that it is essentially that way is simply that the former fact is grounded in the latter fact.[62] And thus the so-called essentialist explanation here is really just a certain kind of grounding explanation. I believe this claim is false, and in Section 2.3 I sketched one of my (2017) arguments against it. If I am right, then essentialist explanation and grounding explanation are two distinct forms of explanation and so this reply fails.

But there is another reply to the Loewer-style response that cannot be dealt with so easily. This is to reply in just the way Lange did: to concede that grounding and essentialist explanation are two distinct forms of explanation but to argue that they chain. If the two halves of the circle chain, then the resulting explanation will violate the principle that explanations must be irreflexive. And so the circularity objection to the origins proposal will succeed after all.

It is important to appreciate that the question of whether grounding and essentialist explanation chain is not trivial. For not all forms of explanation chain. To see this, consider the following case from Glazier (2021). Suppose

---

[61] See Hicks and van Elswyk (2015) and Miller (2015) for challenges, and Marshall (2015) for responses to those challenges.

[62] Such a view is at least floated by Rosen (2010), Kment (2014), and Dasgupta (2016).

a preference satisfaction account of well-being is correct, and suppose that Jones prefers wealth to wisdom. Given the preference satisfaction account, then, wealth is better for Jones than wisdom, and it is plausible to take the fact that wealth is better for Jones than wisdom to be grounded in the fact that Jones prefers wealth to wisdom. There is therefore a grounding explanation of the former in terms of the latter. Yet there may also be an explanation in the other direction. For suppose that the reason Jones offers for why she prefers wealth to wisdom is that wealth is better for her than wisdom. A certain "rational" kind of explanation may thus be given of why Jones prefers wealth to wisdom by citing her reason: wealth is better for her than wisdom. We therefore have an explanatory circle: the better-than fact explains the preference fact and vice versa. If the two halves of this circle chain, then in Langean fashion a violation of irreflexivity would follow. It must be, then, that *these* two forms of explanation, at least, do not chain.

We thus have no choice but to adjudicate questions of chaining case by case. So what should we say about grounding and essentialist explanation? Do they chain?

I will argue that the answer is "no." My strategy will be to consider some candidate chaining principles and argue that they all fail. I cannot consider all possible candidate principles, but I will consider the four most obvious ones. In schematic form, these are:

(1) ⟨essentialist, grounding⟩ → essentialist
(2) ⟨grounding, essentialist⟩ → essentialist
(3) ⟨grounding, essentialist⟩ → grounding
(4) ⟨essentialist, grounding⟩ → grounding

Call the explanations inside the brackets the *links* in the chain and the explanation to the right of the arrow the *result*.

To illustrate, let me give a non-schematic statement of the first of these principles. It will then be clear how to state the other three.

(1) For every *A*, *B*, and *C*, if the fact that *A* provides an essentialist explanation of the fact that *B*, and if the fact that *B* provides a grounding explanation of the fact that *C*, then the fact that *A* provides an essentialist explanation of the fact that *C*.

I have made a simplification in stating this chaining principle. An explanation has an explanans (what does the explaining) as well as an explanandum (what gets explained). And I have assumed that, for each link, its explanans is a single fact. But the explanans of a grounding explanation can also consist of a plurality of facts, as when we explain why Bowser is big-and-bad by citing both the fact that he is big as well as the fact that he is bad. Still, this simplification is harmless for present purposes, and so I will continue to indulge in it below.

Let us now argue against our four chaining principles in turn.

Principle (1): ⟨essentialist, grounding⟩ → essentialist

As I understand essentialist explanation, it obeys certain formal requirements. The explanans of an essentialist explanation is always of the form "t is essentially such that A"; and the explanandum is always of the form "A." So let the explanans of the essentialist link be the fact that t is essentially such that A. Then the explanandum of the essentialist link must be the fact that A. Now the explanandum of the essentialist link is also the explanans of the grounding link. And so the explanandum of the grounding link must be the fact that B, where B is distinct from A (for no fact explains itself). Since the explanans of the putative result is also the explanans of the essentialist link, that explanans is the fact that t is essentially such that A. And since the explanandum of the result is also the explanandum of the grounding link, that explanandum is the fact that B. But since B is distinct from A, the result is not of the proper form to be an essentialist explanation. Thus principle (1) is false.

Principle (2) ⟨grounding, essentialist⟩ → essentialist

As before, the explanans of the essentialist link must be of the proper form; let it again be the fact that t is essentially such that A. The explanandum of the essentialist link must therefore be the fact that A. Since the explanandum of the essentialist link is also the explanandum of the putative result, that explanandum is the fact that A.

Let us suppose for reductio that principle (2) holds and so that the result is an essentialist explanation. Then since its explanandum is the fact that A, there must be some s such that its explanans is the fact that s is essentially such that A. This explanans is also the explanans of the grounding link. And since the explanandum of the grounding link is also the explanans of the essentialist link, that explanandum is the fact that t is essentially such that A. Since no fact explains itself, s and t must be distinct.

Now it is a plausible principle that any proposition which is essential to something must involve that thing.[63] Since t is essentially such that A, A must involve t. And since s is also essentially such that A, A must involve s as well.

---

[63] See Glazier (2017) for a defense of this principle.

Zylstra (2019) objects that one way of generalizing this principle to accommodate cases of collective essence (Section 2.2) fails. He argues that, because singleton Socrates depends on

But this situation leads to an objectionable kind of circular explanation. This is because to say that something is essentially a certain way is to explain, at least in part, what that thing is.[64] For example, since singleton Socrates is essentially a set containing Socrates, we may explain or partly explain what singleton Socrates is by saying that it is a set containing Socrates. Above, we argued that t is essentially such that A, and A involves s; thus what t is may be explained in terms of s (possibly together with some other things). But we also argued that s is essentially such that A, and A involves t; thus what s is may be explained in terms of t.

To be sure, we earlier suggested that, in at least some cases, the existence of an explanatory circle is unproblematic. But those were cases in which the two "halves" of the circle involved different forms of explanation. This case is different. Here both halves involve the same form of explanation: explanation of what something is. And *this* kind of explanatory circle is impossible. We must therefore reject the supposition (made for reductio) that principle (2) holds.

Principle (3): ⟨grounding, essentialist⟩ → grounding

In the final chapter of *Writing the Book of the World* (2011), Ted Sider puts forward "a worldview according to which fundamental reality contains nothing but physics, [classical first-order] logic, and set theory" (292). This is not the radical view that there are no people, or cities, or clouds. The view is simply that these things, though they certainly exist, form no part of fundamental reality.

Now Sider himself understands fundamentality in terms of a certain notion of "metaphysical structure," elaborated over the course of his book. But it does not seem to do violence to the underlying metaphysical vision if we understand fundamentality in a slightly different way, in terms of the notion of ground. We

---

Socrates, we should take it to be essential to Socrates and singleton Socrates *taken together* that singleton Socrates is a set. But the proposition "singleton Socrates is a set" does not involve Socrates, and so Zylstra concludes that a proposition which is essential to some things need not involve all of those things – contrary to the generalized version of the principle. In response, I do not think it is plausibly essential (in the "constitutive" sense both Zylstra and I have in mind) to Socrates and singleton Socrates taken together that the latter is a set (and I do not see why pointing out that singleton Socrates depends on Socrates helps). For the nature of Socrates does not seem to play any role in ensuring that singleton Socrates is a set; the nature of singleton Socrates can do that on its own.

It may help to contrast this case with a case in which the relevant claim of collective essence is less controversial. Consider the claim that it is essential to Socrates and Biden taken together that they are distinct. Here both the nature of Socrates and the nature of Biden seem to play a role in ensuring distinctness. (There may be other senses of essence, not at issue in the present discussion, in which my principle fails; see Fine [1995b].)

[64] This point is made in Glazier (2017); see also Fine (2015: 296–297) as well as the discussion in Section 2.1 of the relationship between essence and what something is.

will take a fact to be fundamental just in case it is not grounded in any other fact. The Siderian worldview, so understood, is in tension with principle (3).

To see why, consider this electron t. It has unit negative charge. And given the Siderian worldview, the fact that t has unit negative charge is plausibly fundamental, for it seems to be a basic fact of physics. Thus on our present understanding of fundamentality, the fact that t has unit negative charge is ungrounded.

At the same time, it is not implausible to think that electrons have the charge they do by their very nature, and so that the particular electron t essentially has unit negative charge. But given the Siderian worldview, the fact that t essentially has unit negative charge cannot be fundamental, for the notion of essence does not belong to physics, classical first-order logic, or set theory. This fact must therefore be grounded in some fundamental fact f.[65]

So the fact f provides a grounding explanation of the fact that t essentially has unit negative charge. And the fact that t essentially has unit negative charge provides an essentialist explanation of the fact that t has unit negative charge. We therefore have the two links of the chain required by principle (3). But we do not have the result: the fact f does not provide a grounding explanation of the fact that t has unit negative charge. For that last fact is ungrounded – it has no grounding explanation at all. And so given the Siderian worldview, there is pressure to reject principle (3).

Of course, this worldview is highly controversial. O'Connor and Montgomery (2013), for example, offer the following criticism:

> [W]e do not at all recognize our world in Sider's stark account: fundamentally a collection of structured spacetime points and sets, accompanied by basic physical predicates and a bit of formal machinery. This is a profoundly anti-humanist vision, in which personhood and value don't merit a mention in the fundamental world book, having no place in the objective deep structure of things.

But although these and other philosophers firmly reject the truth of this worldview, few have suggested it is in tension with basic principles of explanation. Yet it is in tension with principle (3). The natural conclusion to draw is that principle (3) is false.

Principle (4): ⟨essentialist, grounding⟩ → grounding

Consider an object that is essentially in either of two states, while not being essentially in the first state nor essentially in the second state. Let it be the

---

[65] Or some fundamental facts, plural – but we may ignore this complication.

boolean variable foo discussed in Section 2.3. We there supposed that, although this variable is essentially such that it has the value 0 or it has the value 1, it does not essentially have the value 0, and nor does it essentially have the value 1. Indeed, it may have first one value and then the other as the program executes.

Now let A be the statement that foo has the value 0, let B be the statement that foo has the value 1, and let C be the statement that foo has the value -1. Then foo is essentially such that $A \vee B$, and this fact provides an essentialist explanation of the fact that $A \vee B$.

Consider now the disjunctive statement obtained by disjoining $A \vee B$ (itself already a disjunction) with C – i.e. the statement $(A \vee B) \vee C$. For all we know, foo might have the value 0 or the value 1, and so either A or B might be true. But since foo must have one of these two values, the disjunctive statement $A \vee B$ is certainly true. In accordance with the general principle that disjunctive facts are grounded in their obtaining disjuncts (Section 3.1), then, the fact that $A \vee B$ will provide a grounding explanation of the fact that $(A \vee B) \vee C$.

So the fact that foo is essentially such that $A \vee B$ provides an essentialist explanation of the fact that $A \vee B$, and the fact that $A \vee B$ provides a grounding explanation of the fact that $(A \vee B) \vee C$. Principle (4) therefore entails that the fact that foo is essentially such that $A \vee B$ provides a grounding explanation of the fact that $(A \vee B) \vee C$.

But it does not. At least, not if we adopt a plausible assumption concerning the grounds of disjunctive facts. We have already appealed to the principle that disjunctive facts are grounded in their obtaining disjuncts. We now adopt the further assumption that disjunctive facts can *only* be grounded in their obtaining disjuncts, or in whatever grounds those disjuncts. The grounding of a disjunction must, so to speak, proceed by way of the obtaining disjuncts.[66]

Return now to the fact that $(A \vee B) \vee C$. Could it be grounded in the essentialist fact that foo is essentially such that $A \vee B$, as principle (4) requires? Well, the fact that $(A \vee B) \vee C$ has two disjuncts: $A \vee B$ and C. And of these two disjuncts, only $A \vee B$ obtains. So given our assumption, the essentialist fact grounds the fact that $(A \vee B) \vee C$ only if it also grounds the fact that $A \vee B$ – and in turn, the essentialist fact grounds the fact that $A \vee B$ only if it also grounds whichever of its disjuncts happens to obtain. Let us suppose that it is the fact that A which obtains (the argument for B is identical). The essentialist fact, then, can ground the fact that $(A \vee B) \vee C$ only if it also grounds the fact that A, the fact that foo has the value 0.

---

[66] This assumption is a simplified version of the elimination rule for disjunction found in several formal treatments of ground including Fine (2012a), Correia (2017a) and Krämer (2018). The differences between our simplified assumption and this elimination rule do not matter for this argument. See Glazier (2017) for further discussion.

But the essentialist fact does not ground the fact that foo has the value 0. For the essentialist fact obtains necessarily (Section 2.2). And so whatever facts it grounds – whatever facts hold in virtue of it – must also obtain necessarily.[67] Yet the fact that foo has the value 0 obtains only contingently. The essentialist fact, then, cannot ground the fact that A and so it cannot ground the fact that $(A \vee B) \vee C$. Since principle (4) entails that it does ground this last fact, principle (4) is false.

We have now examined the four most obvious chaining principles that might govern grounding and essentialist explanation and have found all wanting. To be sure, we have not shown definitively that grounding and essentialist explanation do not chain, but the prospects for chaining do not look good.

Where does this leave the origins proposal for grounding essentialist facts? The above considerations suggest that the Loewer-style response to the objection should be allowed to stand. The origins proposal, to be sure, does lead to an explanatory circle, but because this circle involves two distinct forms of explanation, the circle as such is unproblematic. And because it seems unlikely that these forms of explanation chain, there is little danger the defender of the origins proposal will face a violation of the principle that explanation is irreflexive.

I conclude that the origins proposal is worth taking seriously. It offers a promising route to grounding a certain class of essentialist facts. And perhaps, with enough reflection and ingenuity, we might even see how to extend this limited proposal into an account of the grounds of essentialist facts more generally.

3.4 Origins and Activity

In this final subsection we return to the question whether essentialist facts are active or latent (Section 1.3). If the origins proposal is correct, does that settle the matter?

It might seem obvious that the answer is "yes." For if essence is somehow grounded in the origins of things, then doesn't it arise from how those things are as opposed to how they might be, must be, were, will be, and so on? And so mustn't essentialist facts turn out to be active?

---

[67] I am here relying on the principle of grounding necessitation: if A grounds B then necessarily, if A then B. This principle is widely held but has sometimes been challenged (notable challenges include Leuenberger [2014] and Skiles [2015a]). A discussion of these challenges lies beyond the scope of this Element.

I think that some argument along these lines may well succeed but that this is far from obvious. One reason is that the origins proposal is limited in scope. It concerns only a certain class of essentialist facts, those of the form "t essentially originated from $s_1, \ldots, s_n$." So even if the proposal could be shown to entail that *these* essentialist facts are active, that would not show that all essentialist facts are. *Perhaps* there is some principle to the effect that all essentialist facts must have the same status with respect to the active/latent distinction, and so if some are active, then all are. To show this to be true, however, would require further argument.

But what if we were somehow able to establish, not just the origins proposal, but the far more general thesis that all essentialist facts are grounded in origin facts, facts of the form "t originated from $s_1, \ldots, s_n$"? This thesis is very closely related to the Almogian thesis of Section 3.2 and faces many of the same difficulties. We have argued that one of these difficulties, the threat of circular explanation, is less worrisome than it initially appears (Section 3.3). But other difficulties still loom. In particular, we have done nothing to address the worry posed by essentialist facts about things that seem to lack origins or that posed by essentialist facts that seem to have nothing to do with origins. I myself am still not prepared to reject the Almogian thesis or indeed the claim that all essentialist facts are grounded in origin facts. But to defend it would seem to be an uphill battle.

Yet let us indulge in the fantasy that the battle has been won. Would it then follow that all essentialist facts are active? We will try to answer this question by seeing whether we can construct an argument to this effect. Here is a first attempt:

(1) All essentialist facts are grounded in origin facts.
(2) All origin facts are active.
(3) Any fact grounded in active facts is itself active.
(4) So all essentialist facts are active.

This argument appears to be valid, but the three premises are highly controversial.

The first we have already discussed; what about the second? One's assessment of it will depend on one's metaphysics of time. For origin facts are, in almost all cases, not facts about the present. And whether such facts are active or latent depends on whether one is an A theorist or a B theorist (Section 1.2). For the B theorist, facts about the past are on a metaphysical par with facts about the present. Thus she will take as active not only facts about present goings-on but also facts about past goings-on, including facts about past events of origination.

But the A theorist will disagree. For her, facts about the past are not on a metaphysical par with facts about the present. Although she will take facts about present goings-on to be active, she will take past origin facts to be latent. They do not concern how things are but only how they were. The only exception to the general latency of origin facts will be those concerning things that are presently originating. Those, and those alone, will be active.

Turning now to the third premise, on a straightforward reading it is clearly false. Consider the active fact that the Eiffel Tower is 984 m tall. Disjunctive facts are grounded in their obtaining disjuncts (Section 3.1), and so this fact grounds the fact that the Eiffel Tower is 984 m tall *or* the virus could have been contained. But this disjunctive fact partly concerns how things could have been, and so it is not active but rather latent.

We may avoid this counterexample by modifying the third premise to be the claim that any fact grounded *only* in active facts is active. For although the disjunctive fact is indeed grounded in the active fact that the Eiffel Tower is 984 m tall, it is also grounded in the latent fact that the virus could have been contained. And so it is not grounded only in active facts.

But a different counterexample may now be given. Consider the disjunctive fact that the Eiffel Tower is 984 m tall or there could have been a greatest prime number. Because its second disjunct concerns what could have been, the disjunctive fact is latent. Yet because it is not a fact that there could have been a greatest prime, the only grounds of the disjunctive fact are active.

There is a way around this counterexample too. It arises because although the disjunct "there could have been a greatest prime" concerns what could have been and is therefore in some sense latent, it does not state a fact, and so its latency does not show up in the grounds of the disjunctive fact. If we could somehow modify the third premise to make it responsive to this kind of consideration, we could avoid the counterexample.

We can achieve this in two steps. First, we have so far understood the active/latent distinction as applying to *facts*. We must now understand the distinction to apply to *propositions* as well. This extension is straightforward: just as the active facts are the facts concerning how things are as opposed to how they might be, must be, were, will be, and so on, so the active propositions are the propositions concerning how things are as opposed to how they might be, must be, were, will be, and so on.

Second, we have so far spoken of some *facts* grounding other *facts*. But we can instead adopt a notion of ground on which it relates *propositions*. Call this the *nonfactive* notion of ground. In this nonfactive sense it will be true, for example, that the proposition that snow is crimson grounds the proposition that snow is red, even though both propositions are false. The idea is roughly that the first proposition, if it were true, would be metaphysically responsible for the truth of the second.[68]

We now modify the third premise to be the claim that any proposition nonfactively grounded only in active propositions is active. On our new propositional understanding of the active/latent distinction, the proposition that there could have been a greatest prime counts as latent. And on our new nonfactive notion of ground, the disjunctive proposition that the Eiffel Tower is 984 m tall or there could have been a greatest prime will be grounded, not only in the active proposition that the Eiffel Tower is 984 m tall, but also in the latent proposition that there could have been a greatest prime. Thus this latest modification of the third premise no longer entails that the disjunctive proposition is active. Counterexample avoided.

Having modified our argument's third premise, we must now modify its other two premises in order to preserve its validity. The most straightforward way of doing this yields the following argument.

(1′) All essentialist propositions are nonfactively grounded only in origin propositions.

(2′) All origin propositions are active.

(3′) Any proposition nonfactively grounded only in active propositions is active.

(4′) So all essentialist propositions are active.

Unfortunately, (1′) is doubtful. For the notion of ground, like the notion of explanation to which it is closely related,[69] is usually taken to be transitive: whatever grounds the grounds of some fact or proposition will *itself* ground that fact or proposition.[70] So if an essentialist proposition is grounded in an origin proposition, then whatever grounds that origin proposition will also ground the essentialist proposition. Yet this further ground may not itself be an origin proposition.

To avoid this objection, we should instead modify the first two premises of the argument in a different way:

---

[68] See Fine (2012a) for further discussion of this and other less commonly encountered notions of ground.

[69] For discussion of the relationship between ground and explanation, see Raven (2015), Dasgupta (2017), and Glazier (2020).

[70] Schaffer (2012) raises a challenge to the transitivity of ground but ultimately accepts it (though he revises other assumptions about ground). Fine (2012a) recognizes a notion of "immediate ground" which is not transitive, but this notion is not at issue in the present discussion.

($1^\dagger$) All essentialist propositions are nonfactively grounded only in origin propositions or in propositions which nonfactively ground origin propositions.

($2^\dagger$) All origin propositions are active, and all propositions which nonfactively ground origin propositions are active.

($3^\dagger$) Any proposition nonfactively grounded only in active propositions is active.

($4^\dagger$) So all essentialist propositions are active.

How does this version of the argument fare?

The modified first premise ($1^\dagger$) adds something to the original first premise (1).[71] Roughly speaking, (1) says that the essentialist facts all arise out of origin facts. And ($1^\dagger$) adds, again roughly speaking, that there is no other way for these facts to arise: the essentialist facts can *only* arise out of origin facts (or their grounds). But although ($1^\dagger$) adds something to (1), it seems that if one has already gone so far as to accept that the essentialist facts all arise out of origin facts, then there is little reason to resist the claim that they can only arise in this way. The two premises (1) and ($1^\dagger$), as far as I can see, are roughly on a par as regards their plausibility or defensibility.

The same is true of (2) and ($2^\dagger$). Roughly speaking, (2) says that all *true* origin propositions are active, and ($2^\dagger$) adds to this the thought that the false ones are too (as well as the grounds of the true and false ones). But if saying something true about origins is saying something concerning how things are as opposed to how they might be, must be, were, will be, and so on, then it seems the same should go for saying something false about origins (or about what grounds origins).

Let us turn now to ($3^\dagger$). As we have seen, it is on a much better footing than (3). For it avoids the straightforward objections faced by the latter. But is it true?

We certainly should not hold, in general, that any proposition which is nonfactively grounded only in propositions of type X is itself of type X. After all, a proposition grounded only in ungrounded propositions is not itself ungrounded.

But even though this general principle is false, its special case ($3^\dagger$) still has a certain plausibility. To see why, suppose someone asks you to consider the proposition that embiggening is cromulent. You have no idea what

---

[71] I do not claim that ($1^\dagger$) is strictly stronger than (1). For suppose that ($1^\dagger$) is true but that all essentialist propositions are nonfactively grounded only in propositions which happen to be false. That is consistent with the actual essentialist facts' lacking (factive) grounds altogether, and so with the falsity of (1).

"embiggening" or "cromulent" mean, but you are told that the only nonfactive grounds for the proposition that embiggening is cromulent are active – they concern how things are as opposed to how they might be, must be, were, will be, and so on. Thus whenever embiggening is cromulent, it is so only in virtue of how things are. And so how could the proposition that embiggening is cromulent fail to concern how things are?

These considerations, however, are not decisive, and it is important to appreciate that $(3^{\dagger})$ is a strong claim. For $(3^{\dagger})$ entails that no latent proposition is nonfactively grounded only in active propositions. This at least suggests that the position articulated by Sider (2003: 184–185) on which the latent facts reduce to the active facts (Section 1.2) is false.[72]

There is much work left to be done in properly assessing the status of $(3^{\dagger})$ and of the argument $(1^{\dagger})$–$(4^{\dagger})$ in which it figures, and we cannot do any more of that work here. Still, I believe this subsection has sketched a promising route from the thought that essences are explained by origins to the conclusion that essence is active. This is progress on, if not a resolution of, the old question whether essence lies within or without our world.

---

[72] See Rosen (2010: 122–126) for discussion of the relationship between reduction and ground.

References

Achinstein, P. 1984. The pragmatic character of explanation. *Proceedings of the Biennial Meeting of the Philosophy of Science Association 1984*: 275–292.

Almog, J. 1989. Logic and the world. *Journal of Philosophical Logic 18*(2): 197–220.

Almog, J. 1991. The what and the how. *Journal of Philosophy 88*(5): 225–244.

Almog, J. 1996. The what and the how II: Reals and mights. *Noûs 30*(4): 413–433.

Almog, J. 1999. Nothing, something, infinity. *Journal of Philosophy 96*(9): 462–478.

Almog, J. 2003. The structure-in-things: Existence, essence and logic. *Proceedings of the Aristotelian Society 103*(2): 197–225.

Almog, J. 2010. Nature without essence. *Journal of Philosophy 107*(7): 360–383.

Amijee, F. 2021. Explaining contingent facts. *Philosophical Studies 178*: 1163–1181.

Aristotle. 1984. *The Complete Works of Aristotle: The Revised Oxford Translation*. Princeton: Princeton University Press.

Armstrong, D. M. 1983. *What is a Law of Nature?* Cambridge: Cambridge University Press.

Ballarin, R. 2013. The necessity of origin: A long and winding route. *Erkenntnis 78*: 353–370.

Bigelow, J., B. Ellis, and C. Lierse. 1992. The world as one of a kind: Natural necessity and the laws of nature. *British Journal for the Philosophy of Science 43*(3): 371–388.

Bird, A. 2007. *Nature's Metaphysics: Laws and Properties*. Oxford: Oxford University Press.

Brody, B. 1980. *Identity and Essence*. Princeton: Princeton University Press.

Brogaard, B. and J. Salerno. 2013. Remarks on counterpossibles. *Synthese 190*: 639–660.

Burgess, J. M. 2020. Kripke on modality. In *Routledge Handbook of Modality*, ed. O. Bueno and S. A. Shalkowski, 400–408. London: Routledge.

Cameron, R. P. 2005. A note on Kripke's footnote 56 argument for the essentiality of origin. *Ratio 18*: 262–275.

Cameron, R. P. 2010. The grounds of necessity. *Philosophy Compass 5*: 348–358.

Charles, D. 2010. Definition and explanation in the *Posterior Analytics* and *Metaphysics*. In *Definition in Greek Philosophy*, ed. D. Charles, 286–328 Oxford: Oxford University Press.

Correia, F. 2005. *Existential Dependence and Cognate Notions*. Munich: Philosophia.

Correia, F. 2006. Generic essence, objectual essence, and modality. *Noûs 40*(4): 753–767.

Correia, F. 2017a. An impure logic of representational grounding. *Journal of Philosophical Logic 46*: 507–538.

Correia, F. 2017b. Real definitions. *Philosophical Issues 27*: 52–73.

Correia, F. Forthcoming. Non-modal conceptions of essence. In *Routledge Handbook of Essence*, ed. M. J. Raven and K. Koslicki. London: Routledge.

Correia, F. and A. Skiles. 2019. Grounding, essence, and identity. *Philosophy and Phenomenological Research 98*(3): 642–670.

Cowling, S. 2013. The modal view of essence. *Canadian Journal of Philosophy 43*(2): 248–266.

Damnjanovic, N. 2010. No route to material origin essentialism? *Erkenntnis 73*: 93–110.

Dasgupta, S. 2014. The possibility of physicalism. *Journal of Philosophy 111*(9): 557–592.

Dasgupta, S. 2015. Inexpressible ignorance. *Philosophical Review 124*(4): 441–480.

Dasgupta, S. 2016. Metaphysical rationalism. *Noûs 50*(2): 379–418.

Dasgupta, S. 2017. Constitutive explanation. *Philosophical Issues 27*: 74–97.

De, M. 2020. A modal account of essence. *Metaphysics 3*(1): 17–32.

Denby, D. 2014. Essence and intrinsicality. In *Companion to Intrinsic Properties*, ed. R. M. Francescotti, 87–109. Berlin: De Gruyter.

Dorr, C. and J. Goodman. 2020. Diamonds are forever. *Noûs 54*(3): 632–665.

Ellis, B. 2001. *Scientific Essentialism*. Cambridge: Cambridge University Press.

Fine, K. 1994. Essence and modality. *Philosophical Perspectives 8*: 1–16.

Fine, K. 1995a. Ontological dependence. *Proceedings of the Aristotelian Society 95*: 269–290.

Fine, K. 1995b. Senses of essence. In *Modality, Morality, and Belief: Essays in Honor of Ruth Barcan Marcus*, ed. W. Sinnott-Armstrong, D. Raffman, and N. Asher, 53–73. Cambridge: Cambridge University Press.

Fine, K. 2000. Semantics for the logic of essence. *Journal of Philosophical Logic 29*: 543–584.

Fine, K. 2002. The varieties of necessity. In *Conceivability and Possibility*, ed. T. S. Gendler and J. Hawthorne, 253–282. Oxford: Oxford University Press.

Fine, K. 2005. Necessity and non-existence. In *Modality and Tense: Philosophical Papers*, 321–354. Oxford: Oxford University Press.

Fine, K. 2012a. Guide to ground. In *Metaphysical Grounding: Understanding the Structure of Reality*, ed. F. Correia and B. Schnieder, 37–80. Cambridge: Cambridge University Press.

Fine, K. 2012b. What is metaphysics? In *Contemporary Aristotelian Metaphysics*, ed. T. E. Tahko, 8–25. Cambridge: Cambridge University Press.

Fine, K. 2013. Fundamental truth and fundamental terms. *Philosophy and Phenomenological Research 88*(3): 725–732.

Fine, K. 2015. Unified foundations for essence and ground. *Journal of the American Philosophical Association 1*(2): 296–311.

Fine, K. 2017a. Naive metaphysics. *Philosophical Issues 27*: 98–113.

Fine, K. 2017b. A theory of truthmaker content II: Subject-matter, common content and ground. *Journal of Philosophical Logic 46*(6): 675–702.

Fine, K. 2020a. Comments on Jessica Wilson's "Essence and Dependence." In *Metaphysics, Meaning, and Modality: Themes from Kit Fine*, ed. M. Dumitru, 471–475. Oxford: Oxford University Press.

Fine, K. 2020b. Comments on Penelope Mackie's "Can Metaphysical Modality Be Based on Essence?" In *Metaphysics, Meaning, and Modality: Themes from Kit Fine*, ed. M. Dumitru, 461–465. Oxford: Oxford University Press.

Gettier, E. L. 1963. Is justified true belief knowledge? *Analysis 23*(6): 121–123.

Glazier, M. 2017. Essentialist explanation. *Philosophical Studies 174*(11): 2871–2889.

Glazier, M. 2020. Explanation. In *The Routledge Handbook of Metaphysical Grounding*, ed. M. J. Raven, 121–132. London: Routledge.

Glazier, M. 2021. The difference between epistemic and metaphysical necessity. *Synthese 198*(6): 1409–1424.

Goodman, N. 1954. *Fact, Fiction, and Forecast*. Cambridge, MA: Harvard University Press.

Gorman, M. 2005. The essential and the accidental. *Ratio 18*(3): 276–289.

Gorman, M. 2014. Essentiality as foundationality. In *Neo-Aristotelian Perspectives in Metaphysics*, ed. D. D. Novotný and L. Novák, 119–137. New York: Routledge.

Hale, B. 2013. *Necessary Beings: An Essay on Ontology, Modality, and the Relations between Them*. Oxford: Oxford University Press.

Hawthorne, J. and T. S. Gendler. 2000. Origin essentialism: The arguments reconsidered. *Mind 109*(434): 285–298.

Hicks, M. T. and P. van Elswyk. 2015. Humean laws and circular explanation. *Philosophical Studies 172*: 433–443.

Johnston, M. 1987. Is there a problem about persistence? *Proceedings of the Aristotelian Society 61*: 107–135.

Kim, J. 1988. Explanatory realism, causal realism, and explanatory exclusion. *Midwest Studies in Philosophy 12*: 225–239.

Kim, J. 1994. Explanatory knowledge and metaphysical dependence. *Philosophical Issues 5*: 51–69.

Kitcher, P. 1981. Explanatory unification. *Philosophy of Science 48*(4): 507–531.

Kment, B. 2014. *Modality and Explanatory Reasoning*. Oxford: Oxford University Press.

Kment, B. 2021. Essence and modal knowledge. *Synthese 198*: 1957–1979.

Koslicki, K. 2012. Varieties of ontological dependence. In *Metaphysical Grounding: Understanding the Structure of Reality*, ed. F. Correia and B. Schnieder, 186–213. Cambridge: Cambridge University Press.

Koslicki, K. 2013. Ontological dependence: An opinionated survey. In *Varities of Dependence: Ontological Dependence, Grounding, Supervenience, Response-Dependence*, ed. M. Hoeltje, B. Schnieder, and A. Steinberg, 31–64. Munich: Philosophia.

Krämer, S. 2018. Towards a theory of ground-theoretic content. *Synthese 195*: 785–814.

Kripke, S. A. 1980. *Naming and Necessity*. Cambridge, MA: Harvard University Press.

Lange, M. 2013. Grounding, scientific explanation, and Humean laws. *Philosophical Studies 164*(1): 255–261.

Leech, J. 2018. Essence and mere necessity. *Royal Institute of Philosophy Supplements 82*: 309–332.

Leech, J. 2021. From essence to necessity via identity. *Mind 130*(519): 887–908.

Leuenberger, S. 2014. Grounding and necessity. *Inquiry 57*(2): 151–174.

Lewis, D. 1973. *Counterfactuals*. Oxford: Blackwell.

Lewis, D. 1986. *On the Plurality of Worlds*. Oxford: Blackwell.

Loewer, B. 2012. Two accounts of laws and time. *Philosophical Studies 160*(1): 115–137.

Lowe, E. J. 2008. Two notions of being: Entity and essence. *Royal Institute of Philosophy Supplements 83*(62): 23–48.

Lowe, E. J. 2012a. Essence and ontology. In *Metaphysics: Aristotelian, Scholastic, Analytic*, ed. L. Novák, D. D. Novotný, P. Sousedík, and D. Svoboda, 93–112. Heusenstamm: Ontos Verlag.

Lowe, E. J. 2012b. What is the source of our knowledge of modal truths? *Mind 121*(484): 919–950.

Lowe, E. J. 2013. *Forms of Thought: A Study in Philosophical Logic*. Cambridge: Cambridge University Press.

Lowe, E. J. 2014. Essence vs. intuition: An unequal contest. In *Intuitions*, ed. A. R. Booth and D. P. Rowbottom, 256–268. Oxford: Oxford University Press.

Mackie, P. 2020. Can metaphysical modality be based on essence? In *Metaphysics, Meaning, and Modality: Themes from Kit Fine*, ed. M. Dumitru, 247–264. Oxford: Oxford University Press.

Mallozzi, A., A. Vaidya, and M. Wallner. 2021. The epistemology of modality. In *The Stanford Encyclopedia of Philosophy* (Fall 2021 ed.), ed. E. N. Zalta. Metaphysics Research Lab, Stanford University. https://plato.stanford.edu/archives/fall2021/entries/modality-epistemology/

Marshall, D. 2015. Humean laws and explanation. *Philosophical Studies 172*: 3145–3165.

Maudlin, T. 2007. *The Metaphysics within Physics*. Oxford: Oxford University Press.

Miller, E. 2015. Humean scientific explanation. *Philosophical Studies 172*: 1311–1332.

O'Connor, T. and N. Montgomery. 2013. Writing the book of the world. *Notre Dame Philosophical Reviews*. https://ndpr.nd.edu/reviews/writing-the-book-of-the-world/

Olson, E. T. 2021. Personal identity. In *The Stanford Encyclopedia of Philosophy* (Spring 2021 ed.), ed. E. N. Zalta. Metaphysics Research Lab, Stanford University. https://plato.stanford.edu/archives/sum2022/entries/identity-personal/

Plato. 1997. *Complete Works*. Indianapolis: Hackett.

Politis, V. 2021. *Plato's Essentialism: Reinterpreting the Theory of Forms*. Cambridge: Cambridge University Press.

Quine, W. V. 1943. Notes on existence and necessity. *Journal of Philosophy 40*(5): 113–127.

Quine, W. V. 1966. Three grades of modal involvement. In *The Ways of Paradox and Other Essays*, 156–174. New York: Random House.

Raven, M. J. 2015. Ground. *Philosophy Compass 10*(5): 322–333.

Raven, M. J. 2020a. Is logic out of this world? *Journal of Philosophy 117*(10): 557–577.

Raven, M. J. (ed.). 2020b. *The Routledge Handbook of Metaphysical Grounding*. London: Routledge.

Raven, M. J. 2021. Explaining essences. *Philosophical Studies 178*: 1043–1064.

Raven, M. J. 2022. A puzzle for social essences. *Journal of the American Philosophical Association 8*(1): 128–148.

Robertson, T. 1998. Possibilities and the arguments for origin essentialism. *Mind 107*(428): 729–749.

Rohrbaugh, G. and L. deRosset. 2004. A new route to the necessity of origin. *Mind 113*: 705–725.

Rosen, G. 2010. Metaphysical dependence: Grounding and reduction. In *Modality: Metaphysics, Logic, and Epistemology*, ed. B. Hale and A. Hoffmann, 109–136. Oxford: Oxford University Press.

Rosen, G. 2015. Real definition. *Analytic Philosophy 56*(3): 189–209.

Ruben, D.-H. 1990. *Explaining Explanation*. London: Routledge.

Salmon, N. 1979. How *not* to derive essentialism from the theory of reference. *Journal of Philosophy 76*(12): 703–725.

Sartre, J.-P. 2007. *Existentialism is a Humanism*. New Haven: Yale University Press.

Schaffer, J. 2008. Causation and laws of nature: Reductionism. In *Contemporary Debates in Metaphysics*, ed. T. Sider, J. Hawthorne, and D. W. Zimmerman, 82–108. Oxford: Blackwell.

Schaffer, J. 2012. Grounding, transitivity, and contrastivity. In *Metaphysical Grounding: Understanding the Structure of Reality*, ed. F. Correia and B. Schnieder, 122–138. Cambridge: Cambridge University Press.

Schnieder, B. 2006. A certain kind of trinity: Dependence, substance, explanation. *Philosophical Studies 129*: 393–419.

Shields, C. 2019. Plato and Aristotle in the academy. In *The Oxford Handbook of Plato* (2nd ed.), ed. G. Fine, 645–667. Oxford: Oxford University Press.

Shimony, A. 1948. The status and nature of essences. *Review of Metaphysics 1*(3): 38–79.

Shoemaker, S. 1980. Causality and properties. In *Time and Cause: Essays Presented to Richard Taylor*, ed. P. van Inwagen, 109–135. Dordrecht: Reidel.

Sidelle, A. 1989. *Necessity, Essence, and Individuation: A Defense of Conventionalism*. Ithaca: Cornell University Press.

Sider, T. 2001. *Four-Dimensionalism: An Ontology of Persistence and Time*. Oxford: Oxford University Press.

Sider, T. 2003. Reductive theories of modality. In *The Oxford Handbook of Metaphysics*, ed. M. J. Loux and D. W. Zimmerman, 180–208. Oxford: Oxford University Press.

Sider, T. 2007. Parthood. *Philosophical Review 116*: 51–91.

Sider, T. 2011. *Writing the Book of the World.* Oxford: Oxford University Press.

Sider, T. 2020. *The Tools of Metaphysics and the Metaphysics of Science.* Oxford: Oxford University Press.

Simons, P. 1987. *Parts: A Study in Ontology.* Oxford: Oxford University Press.

Skiles, A. 2015a. Against grounding necessitarianism. *Erkenntnis 80*: 717–751.

Skiles, A. 2015b. Essence in abundance. *Canadian Journal of Philosophy 45*(1): 100–112.

Sullivan, M. 2017. Are there essential properties? No. In *Current Controversies in Metaphysics*, ed. E. Barnes, 45–61. London: Routledge.

Tahko, T. E. 2017. Empirically-informed modal rationalism. In *Modal Epistemology after Rationalism*, ed. R. W. Fischer and F. Leon, 29–45. Dordrecht: Springer.

Tahko, T. E. 2018. The epistemology of essence. In *Ontology, Modality, Mind: Themes from the Metaphysics of E. J. Lowe*, ed. A. Carruth, S. C. Gibb, and J. Heil, 93–110. Oxford: Oxford University Press.

Tahko, T. E. and E. J. Lowe. 2020. Ontological dependence. In *The Stanford Encyclopedia of Philosophy* (Fall 2020 ed.), ed. E. N. Zalta. Metaphysics Research Lab, Stanford University. https://plato.stanford.edu/archives/fall2020/entries/dependence-ontological/

Taylor, E. 2017. Against explanatory realism. *Philosophical Studies 175*(1): 197–219.

van Fraassen, B. C. 1980. *The Scientific Image.* Oxford: Oxford University Press.

Wiggins, D. 2001. *Sameness and Substance Renewed.* Cambridge: Cambridge University Press.

Wildman, N. 2013. Modality, sparsity, and essence. *Philosophical Quarterly 63*(253): 760–782.

Williamson, T. 2013. *Modal Logic as Metaphysics.* Oxford: Oxford University Press.

Wilson, J. 2020. Essence and dependence. In *Metaphysics, Meaning, and Modality: Themes from Kit Fine*, ed. M. Dumitru, 283–300. Oxford: Oxford University Press.

Yablo, S. 2014. *Aboutness.* Princeton: Princeton University Press.

Zylstra, J. 2019. Collective essence and monotonicity. *Erkenntnis 84*: 1087–1101.

Acknowledgments

I would like to thank Fatema Amijee, Singa Behrens, Stephan Krämer, Mike Raven, Stefan Roski, and the participants of a 2021 workshop on relevance, explanation, and ground held somewhere in cyberspace between Hamburg, Geneva, and Louvain for discussion, comments, inspiration, and encouragement. My thanks also to the series editor Tuomas Tahko as well as to two referees for Cambridge for many detailed comments and suggestions. I am grateful for the support of the German Research Foundation and the Swiss National Science Foundation.

Cambridge Elements

Metaphysics

Tuomas E. Tahko
University of Bristol

Tuomas E. Tahko is Professor of Metaphysics of Science at the University of Bristol, UK. Tahko specializes in contemporary analytic metaphysics, with an emphasis on methodological and epistemic issues: 'meta-metaphysics'. He also works at the interface of metaphysics and philosophy of science: 'metaphysics of science'. Tahko is the author of *Unity of Science* (Cambridge University Press, 2021, *Elements in Philosophy of Science*), *An Introduction to Metametaphysics* (Cambridge University Pres, 2015) and editor of *Contemporary Aristotelian Metaphysics* (Cambridge University Pres, 2012).

About the Series

This highly accessible series of Elements provides brief but comprehensive introductions to the most central topics in metaphysics. Many of the Elements also go into considerable depth, so the series will appeal to both students and academics. Some Elements bridge the gaps between metaphysics, philosophy of science, and epistemology.

Cambridge Elements ≡

Metaphysics